# SPIRITUAL GIFTS

## BIBLE STUDY NOTES

To: Valerie Neil
Thanks For Your
Support.

### HERROL J. SADLER

Palmetto Publishing Group
Charleston, SC

SPIRITUAL GIFTS
Copyright © 2019 by Herrol J. Sadler

First Edition

Printed in the United States

ISBN-13: 978-1-64111-428-8
ISBN-10: 1-64111-428-2

# CONTENTS

PREFACE ···························································· v
INTRODUCTION ················································· vii

Chapter 1    ADMINISTRATION ····························· 1
Chapter 2    APOSTLE ·············································· 6
Chapter 3    CELIBACY ············································· 11
Chapter 4    DISCERNMENT ···································· 14
Chapter 5    EVANGELISM ······································ 20
Chapter 6    EXHORTATION ···································· 25
Chapter 7    FAITH ·················································· 32
Chapter 8    GIVING ················································ 38
Chapter 9    HEALING ·············································· 42
Chapter 10   HOSPITALITY ······································ 50
Chapter 11   MIRACLES ············································ 53
Chapter 12   PASTORS ·············································· 56
Chapter 13   PROPHECY ··········································· 65
Chapter 14   TEACHING ··········································· 76
Chapter 15   WORD OF KNOWLEDGE ······················ 85
Chapter 16   WORD OF WISDOM ···························· 91
Chapter 17   TONGUES ············································ 96
Chapter 18   INTERPRETATION OF TONGUES ········· 103
Chapter 19   WRAP-UP ············································ 107
Chapter 20   QUESTION & ANSWERS ······················ 110

CLOSING ··························································· 120
REFERENCES ····················································· 121
ABOUT THE AUTHOR ········································ 123

# PREFACE

During my early life as a Christian, I had considerable struggles with the subject of Spiritual Gifts. I had numerous question and few answers. Does everyone have a Spiritual Gift? Do I have a Spiritual Gift? How do I know what my Spiritual Gift is? How does the gift manifest itself? Do I automatically receive the gift once I receive the Holy Spirit, or is it developed afterwards? If I don't use it, do I lose it? With the passage of time and with ongoing illumination from the Holy Spirit, and having gained considerably more experience, knowledge and understanding of biblical teachings, I can now speak with some assurance to the questions that I had and to the subject as a whole.

Today, during my daily interactions with members in the local church and throughout Christendom, I realize many are experiencing the same struggles that I had as a young Christian. They do not have a grasp of the working of Spiritual Gifts. Like I did, they have many questions. Some have even expressed frustration at their inability to know their spiritual gift and how to harness it to serve the body of Christ.

Commencing in February 2017, the Lord directed that bible study in our local church focus on tackling this difficult, but important subject. With time, interest in the study grew considerably and took on a life of its own. It became clear that I needed to find a way to broaden the base of those who stand to benefit from the study. With that, I decided to convert the bible study notes into a format that can be made available and shared with others who are unable to participate in our weekly bible studies. The resulting compilation has given birth to *"Bible Study Notes on Spiritual Gifts"* as presented in this booklet. It is in fact notes that are extracted from Bible Studies that took place in Church, during 2017.

The presentation and style is not to be considered as a theological treatment of the subject. Rather, it is intended to be more conversational and practical. It is intended to be viewed in the same way a teacher would present the subject while standing in front of a class. It provides guidelines to individuals who are still in search of their spiritual gift or those who seek general understanding of the subject as a whole. Even if you are comfortable with your knowledge and grasp of this subject, it provides tips and guidelines to enhance your ministry.

At the end of this study I have added a brief section with Questions and Answers. While this section is added mainly to replicate the bible study setting, it also attempts to address some burning questions that the reader may have had. The questions selected are not hypothetical or fictitious and are not intended to resolve all questions that will inevitably arise when studying this subject. Instead, they are real questions that members of the congregation asked during bible study.

I hope that the reader will find answers to some of the questions they have had for many years. Also, I trust that even if you have not discovered what is your spiritual gift after reading the material presented here, you will be more enlightened on this subject, and continue to pursue your search, only this time you will have a considerably greater level of understanding.

# INTRODUCTION

The Ministry of Jesus Christ interrupted a period of Prophetic Silence (*called the 400 silent years*). At long last, the silence was broken. Scriptures proclaimed:

> "*The voice of one crying in the wilderness, prepare ye the way of the Lord, make his paths straight.*" (Matthew 3:3).

John The Baptist emerged, in the same vein of an old prophet, but to usher in a new Dispensation – *The Dispensation of Grace.* This new dispensation was significantly different from the Old. How different? - In the old dispensation, the law was based on commandments written on tables of stone. The new Dispensation is based on God writing the laws on the fleshy tables of the heart.

John characterized the new dispensation by stating:

> "*He that cometh after me, is mightier than I. He shall baptize you with the Holy Ghost and with fire.*" (Matthew 3:11).

As later outlined in the Gospels, Jesus established his Ministry and proceeded to accomplish his mission in a way not previously revealed in the Old Testament scriptures (except in *Types*). As an example, the first official presentation Jesus made to the Jews is the Olivet Discourse outlined in St. Matthew 5-7, during which he carefully explained the constitution of the Kingdom in the New Order. In addition, when he came to John at Jordan to be baptized, he made it very clear in response to John's question and comment that his Baptism was to "*fulfill all righteousness.*" (Matthew 3:15).

Jesus' teaching on the Kingdom of Heaven was new to Israel. Some were mystified by this teaching as evidenced by the question that they asked:

> *"Now when John had heard in prison the work of Christ, he sent two of his disciples, and said unto him, are thou he that should come, or do we look for another?"*
> (St. Matthew11:2).

On other occasions Jesus referred to the Kingdom as:

*"Righteousness, Peace and Joy in the Holy Ghost"* as well, elsewhere he stated that his *"kingdom is not of this world"* and:

> *"From the days of John the Baptist until now the Kingdom of heaven suffereth violence, and the violent take it by force."*
> (Matthew 11:12)

Towards the end of his earthly ministry, the Disciples questioned him saying:

> *"Lord wilt thou at this time restore again the Kingdom to Israel?"*
> (Acts 1:6).

So, Jesus' ministry was different from what Israel, or others had seen previously.

The Old Testament was characterized by God conveying his will through statutes, commandments and precepts, with the Law of Moses as the focal point. Notice that God spoke to Noah, Abraham, Isaac, Jacob, Moses, Joshua, Judges, Kings and Prophets.

In the New Testament, Jesus demonstrated a completely new way how God would work. Through the proclamation of the Gospel, he confirmed all his words and actions by signs (*distinguishing feature by which one is identified*) and wonders (*something so unusual that it requires close watching or observation*). Not only did he confirm his own words and actions but he confirmed much of what the Old Testament prophets had said about him. Also, he fulfilled those things which were written about him and things that referred to him in *types* and *shadows*.

Jesus made it very clear what his mission on earth was, judging how he called the disciples to himself.

> "*When they had heard what great things he did,*
> *came unto him… For he had healed many, insomuch*
> *that they pressed upon him for to touch him, as man*
> *as had plagues. And unclean spirits, when they saw him,*
> *fell down before him, and cried saying art thou the son*
> *of God.*" (St. Mark 3:8-11).

Having performed these great miracles by demonstration, he called his disciples.

> "*And he ordained twelve, that they should be with him,*
> *and that he might send them forth to preach and to have*
> *power to heal sicknesses, and to cast out devils.*"
> (Mark 3:14-15).

In calling and appointing twelve disciples, Jesus Christ first authorized them to go preach (proclaim for God) the gospel of the Kingdom. This was no doubt an extension of himself so the work of the kingdom may be accomplished.

> "*Thy kingdom come, thy will be done in earth, as it is in*
> *heaven.*" (Matthew 6:10).

Christ appointed the disciples as his Agent in the earth. In so doing he gives them the rights and privilege that he himself holds (similar to *Power of Attorney*).

The only way man can represent God, is if man has the spirit of God in him. So, in effect Christ dispersed his spirit through his disciples that they could do exactly as he would do.

Mind you, they did not receive the spirit of God then (as ultimately intended, as that would happen later, on the *Day of Pentecost*), simply put, they executed a "limited" restricted mission. Notice how Jesus gave the selected disciples the scope of the mission, and what was their restriction.

> *"Go not in the way of the Gentiles, and into any city of the Samaritans enter ye not. But go rather to the lost sheep of the house of Israel. And as ye go, preach, saying the kingdom of heaven is at hand. Heal the sick, cleanse the lepers, raise the dead, cast out devils: freely ye have received, freely give. Provide neither gold, nor silver, nor brass in your purses, nor scrip for your journey, neither two coats, neither shoes, nor yet staves: for the workman is worthy of his meat."* (Matthew 10:5-10).

Later, in anticipation of them being filled with the Holy Spirit, Jesus expanded the mission of his disciples. This time, he removed the restrictions that had previously been placed on the disciples. Here are some examples:

> *"Verily I say unto you, whatsoever ye shall bind on earth shall be bound in heaven: and whatsoever ye shall loose on earth shall be loosed in heaven."* (Matthew 18:18).

> *"But ye shall receive power after that the Holy Ghost is come upon you, and ye shall be witness unto me, both in Jerusalem and*

*in all Judea and in Samaria, and unto the uttermost part of the earth."* (Acts 1:8).

The Gifts of the Spirit will be discussed in alphabetical order in the chapters that follow. I invite you to take the journey with me.

# CHAPTER ONE

# ADMINISTRATION

*"And God hath set some in the church, first apostles, secondarily prophets, thirdly teachers, after that miracles, then gifts of healings, helps, governments, diversities of tongues."* (I Corinthians 12:28).

*"To Titus, mine own son after the common faith: Grace, mercy, and peace, from God the Father and the Lord Jesus Christ our Saviour; For this cause left I thee in Crete, that thou shouldest set in order the things that are wanting, and ordain elders in every city, as I had appointed thee:"* (Titus 1:4-5).

## Gift Definition

**The Spiritual Gift of Administration is exercised by those who possess and offers wise Godly council to church leaders and is involved with the governance that supports the decisions of church leadership.**

---

The word administration is derived from the Greek word *Kubernesis.* This is a term that refers to a shipmaster or captain, and means one who Steers, Rule or Govern.

Its meaning conveys the idea of someone who guides and directs a group of people toward a goal or destination. A variation of this word is seen in the following scripture text:

> "*Nevertheless, the centurion believed the master and owner of the ship, more than those things which were spoken by Paul*" (Acts 27:11)

> "*For in one hour so great riches is come to nought. And every shipmaster and all the company in the ships, and sailors, and as many as trade by the sea, stood afar off.*" *(Rev. 18:17)*.

From the definition of kubernesis, we conclude that those who operate in the gift of administration steers the body of Christ towards the accomplishments of God-given goals and direction by planning, organizing and supervising others. The focus of one who operates in this gift is on the resources within the church organization and not so much on managing people.

A great example of the exercise of the gift of administration is seen in Apostle Paul`s instruction to Titus:

> "*To Titus, mine own son after the common faith: Grace, mercy and peace, from God the father and Lord Jesus Christ our saviour. For this cause left I thee in Crete, that thou shouldest set in order the things that are wanting, and ordain elders in every city, as I had appointed thee.*" (Titus 1:4-5).

Those who operate in this gift typically are good organizers, and have the ability to see the big picture without overlooking small details. Because of the big picture view of this gift, it is more quickly noticed to be at work among Pastors, Elders, other church officials and is strongly related to other leadership gifts.

Notwithstanding, this gift is not to be restricted to pastors and church leaders. Many lay members often possess this gift, and some even work in administrative positions in their secular work.

Other persons who would benefit greatly from this gift are church auxiliary leaders such as: Youth Leaders, Men and Women's Group leaders, Sunday School Superintendent and Children's Ministry Coordinators.

Here is a list of some of the key skills, techniques and attributes that are associated with the efficient exercise of this gift. The reader can use this list to assess whether this gifting is in them and may wish to develop this gift further:

&dagger; Adept at Coordinating Events

&dagger; Pays attention to details

&dagger; Good at getting things done

&dagger; Follow-up

&dagger; Good at Event Planning and Organizing

&dagger; Adept at developing or contributing to Learning Curriculum

&dagger; Director of Christian Education including New Converts Program

&dagger; Skill in getting Ministries off the ground

&dagger; Organizing or Developing Church Organization Structure

For those who have an interest in Administration or believe they have this gift, here are some things that you can do:

- † Learn to manage yourself. Those that possess this gift are themselves organized

- † Acquire and read textbooks or written material on development of organizational skills. Do not restrict your reading to religious literature only. There are excellent materials in the secular world

- † Read about Organizational Structure and how they work, which structure is more suited for situations that apply to your church or ministry

- † You will find that the development of your motivational skills is beneficial

- † Time management skill is a great asset to your craft

- † Communication skill is indispensable and should be in your toolkit

- † Department or Auxiliary leaders should be exposed to Organizational and Leadership development

- † Be prepared to share acquired organizational skills with others

- † Volunteering is a great way to help to develop needed skills

- † Be teachable and open to learning

- † A disorganized church is one where the Gift of Administration is lacking

† There is a systematic way to get things done. What is that system?

Here are some keywords to use in your search for information on this Gift that will be beneficial:

1.  Leadership in Christian Ministries

2.  Leadership Styles

3.  Management and Administration

Finally, as the Administrator you are the driver of the vehicle in which others are passengers.

† You determine the destination. If you do not know the destination, you must have the information how to get there, or where to get the help.

† You determine the vehicle that is used to get to the destination. The choice of vehicle will depend on the number of passengers and what is the level of comfort you desire.

† You determine the route. Sometimes, the shortest route is preferred. Other times a more scenic route is desired especially if time is not a constraint. However, if you take the scenic route, you will use more fuel. Be prepared.

CHAPTER TWO

# APOSTLE

*"And he gave some, apostles; and some, prophets; and some, evangelists; and some, pastors and teachers."* (Ephesians 4:11).

*"And God hath set some in the church, first apostles, secondarily prophets, thirdly teachers, after that miracles, then gifts of healings, helps, governments, diversities of tongues."* (I Corinthians 12:28).

## Gift Definition

**One sent forth with the Gospel to new frontiers providing leadership over churches and maintaining authority over spiritual matters.**

---

The word Apostle is derived from the Greek noun – Apostolos: Apollo – from, Stello – send. Hence, one sent forth.

A careful study of this gift leads to the conclusion that there is a difference between the spiritual gift of Apostleship, and the office of the Apostle. Based on scripture, the office of the Apostle was held by a limited number of men, chosen by Jesus Christ. These include twelve disciples as follows:

> *"And he goeth up into a mountain and called unto him whom he would: and they came unto him. And he ordained twelve, that they should be with him, and that he might send them forth to preach and to have power to heal sickness, and to cast out devils. And Simon he surnamed Peter, and James and the son of Zebedee, and John, the brother of James, and he surnamed them Boanerges which is, the Son of Thunder. And Andrew and Philip, and Bartholomew, and Matthew, and Thomas, and James the son of Alpheus, and Thaddaeus, and Simon the Canaanite, and Judas Iscariot, which also betrayed him: and they went into a house."* (St. Mark 3:13-19).

Let us revisit the definition of the Apostle as one sent forth to new frontiers with the gospel. With the emphasis on the new frontiers, this refers to areas not previously exposed to the gospel. Since the apostle was the one who explored new churches, regions and countries, part of their role was to oversee the new churches and set up pastors and elders. This gave rise to a 2-fold duty of an apostle. Jesus empowered the apostles:

> *"But ye shall receive power after that the holy ghost is come upon you and ye shall be witnesses unto me, both in Jerusalem and in all Judea and in Samaria, even unto the uttermost part of the earth."* (Acts 1:8).

Notice here that the apostles were those tasked with bringing the gospel to all classes of people in the earth; to the Jews – Jerusalem, Samaritans – Samaria and Gentiles – uttermost part of the earth.

The apostles who Jesus sent forth were to serve as Witnesses of his resurrection, as they proclaim the Gospel of Jesus Christ. Given that the gospel of Christ is the "Good News of his Death, Burial and Resurrection," it was essential that those proclaiming that message were able to bear witness of that fact. Notice that, in his first sermon following the advent of the Holy Ghost on the day of Pentecost,

## Peter established Jesus' death:

> "*Him, being delivered by the determinate counsel and foreknowledge of God, ye have taken, and by wicked hands have crucified and slain:*" (Acts 2:23);

## Peter established Jesus' resurrection:

> "*Whom God hath raised up, having loosed the pains of death: because it was not possible that he should be holden of it.*" (Acts 2:24);

## Peter established that they were witnesses:

> "*This Jesus hath God raised up, whereof we all are witnesses.*" (Acts 2:32)

Paul, in his letter to the Corinthians, went to great length to establish the many eyewitnesses to Jesus' resurrection as follows:

> "*For I delivered unto you first of all that which I also received, how that Christ died for our sins according to the scriptures: and that he was buried, and that he rose again the third day to the scriptures: and that he was seen of Cephas, then of the twelve: after that, he was seen of above five hundred brethren at once; of whom the greater part remain unto this present, but some are fallen asleep. After that, he was seen of James then of all the apostles. And last of all he was seen of me.*" also, as of one born out of due time.* (I Corinthians 15:3-8)

Paul went on to establish that the witness to Christ's resurrection is critical to the gospel message, by stating:

> *"And if Christ be not risen, then is our preaching vain, and your faith is also vain. Yea, and we are found false witnesses of God; because we have testified of God that he raised up Christ: whom he raised not up, if so be that the dead rise not."*
> (I Corinthians 15:14-15).

The apostles' witness was not merely testimony about their personal beliefs. They testified about the events they personally witnessed.

> *"That which was from the beginning, which we have heard, which we have seen with our eyes, which we have looked upon, and our hands have handled, of the Word of life; (For the life was manifested, and we have seen it, and bear witness, and shew unto you that eternal life, which was with the Father, and was manifested unto us;)*
>
> *That which we have seen and heard declare we unto you, that ye also may have fellowship with us: and truly our fellowship is with the Father, and with his Son Jesus Christ. And these things write we unto you, that your joy may be full."* (I John 1:1-4).

Notice that when the apostles gathered together to elect one to fill the vacancy that Judas had left (having betrayed Christ), they outlined the criteria.

> *"Wherefore of these men which have companied with us all the time that the Lord Jesus went in and out among us, beginning from the baptism of John, unto that same day that he was taken up from us, must one be ordained to be a witness with us of his resurrection."* (Acts 1:21-22).

The primary concern of the early church is that those who were sent had the ability to provide eyewitness evidence regarding the resurrection of Jesus. Peter confirmed this when speaking to Cornelius about his duties, as follows:

> *"And we are witnesses of all things which he did both in the land of the Jews, and in Jerusalem, whom they slew and hanged on a tree: Him God raised up the third day, and shewed him openly, Not to all the people, but unto witnesses chosen before God, even to us, who did eat and drink with him after he rose from the dead."* (Acts 10:39-41).

It is important to understand that these men were not self-appointed missionaries. They were sent by Jesus Christ himself, hence the name "Apostle."

It is of interest to note that we often speak of witnessing for Christ. In the strictest sense, we cannot be witnesses. We were not present when Christ walked this earth. We did not see him die. We are not witnesses of his resurrection. Instead, we can give evidence of the change Christ has made in our own lives once we become converted.

The major distinction between the church today and the Apostles is that they were physically with Christ. They can offer their personal testimony concerning what they witnessed (what they saw and what they heard).

# CHAPTER THREE
# CELIBACY

*"For I would that all men were even as I myself. But every man hath his proper gift of God, one after this manner, and another after that."* (I Corinthians 7:7-9).

## Gift Definition

**To voluntarily remain single without regret and with the ability to maintain controlled sexual impulses so as to serve the Lord without distraction.[1]**

---

The word celibacy did not originate from the apostles and was not used in the first century church. It appears that word crept into prominence due to the influence of Roman Catholicism. The Roman Catholic church took a stand in favor of celibacy in the twelfth century at the second Lateran Council, held in 1139, when a rule was approved forbidding priests to marry. In 1563 the council of Trent reaffirmed this tradition of celibacy.

The reader may be somewhat surprised to see this subject amongst the listings of Spiritual Gifts. However, it is treated briefly in this study because Apostle Paul addressed it in his letter to the Corinthians:

*"For I would that all men were even as I myself. But everyman hath his proper gift of God, one after this manner, and another after that. I say therefore to the unmarried and widows, it is good for them if they abide even as I. But if they cannot contain, let them marry: For it is better to marry than to burn."*
(I Corinthians 7:7-9).

*"The wife hath not power of her own body, but the husband: and likewise also the husband hath not power of his own body, but the wife"* (I Corinthians 7:4).

It is clear that those who are married have a duty to their spouse, and so cannot commit totally to God. The only guarantee one can meaningfully pledge totally and completely to God is through a covenant with God. This is referred to *(in Catholicism)* as a vow of celibacy.

In marriage, the principal duty of a husband to his wife is to love her. The principal duty of a wife to her husband is to submit to him. These principal duties may conflict with a need to commit wholly and solely to God, so celibacy seeks to ensure such conflicts are eliminated.

In an age characterized by sexual libertinism, perversion and endless opportunities for illicit sex, the ability to insulate oneself from lust and sexual indulgence is a noteworthy accomplishment in and of itself. In the electronic age, it is difficult to browse the internet without pornographic websites and dating sites pop-ups. How many times have you seen sites trying to attract you the viewer to *"young Asian beauties"* or something similar? The systems of the world have made it easy and convenient to appeal to the lust of the flesh. In the past, a person had to carefully search out these nefarious magazines and opportunities. Now it is readily available in the *"palm of your hand."*

Schools have made it more convenient for students to experiment with sex by providing birth control facilities and guaranteeing students with protecting their identity and activity against their parents or other responsible adults. Against that backdrop, it requires a special gifting to abstain from sexual indulgence.

To consciously and deliberately dedicate oneself to God, at the exclusion of such indulgence is indeed a Gift. Many have professed to abstain from such indulgence only to be found participating in sexual relations illicitly. The ongoing change in the Roman Catholic Church, where members of the clergy who previously swore to celibacy have now been exposed for engaging in non-consensual, illicit sexual encounters much to the outcry of the wider society.

In an article from CNN dated February 6, 2019 [2], "**Aboard the papal plane**" the article states:

> For the first time, Pope Francis has acknowledged the sexual abuse of nuns by priests and bishops as a 'problem' in the Catholic Church, saying that "we've been working on this for some time.

Sexual impropriety even among those who are married is pervasive within the broader Christian community and even within evangelical churches, both lay persons and clergy. With the obvious challenges of *bridling lust* (exercising self-control), those like Apostle Paul, who pledge them self to celibacy, for Christ's sake is exercising a special gift. They are enabled to continue in this gift only by the Spirit.

For those who faithfully operate in this gift, they can be an invaluable resource and asset to the church. Some of the areas they can be effective in include:

✝ Building and strengthening a Singles Ministry
✝ Offer services in Support Ministries such as Counselling
✝ Deliverance Ministry – Sex and Addiction

C H A P T E R   F O U R
# DISCERNMENT

*"To another the working of miracles; to another prophecy; to another discerning of spirits; to another divers kinds of tongues; to another the interpretation of tongues:"* (I Corinthians 12:10).

## Gift Definition

**To clearly distinguish truth from error by judging whether a behavior or teaching is from God or from the devil, human error or human power.**

---

The writer feels strongly that everyone who has the spirit of God does have a measure of discernment. The ability to; by the spirit, detect error. This is based on the fact that God is light and in him there is no darkness. As a result, the presence of light automatically dispels darkness in all forms. So, even without the full gift of Discernment at work, every spirit filled believer possess a measure of discernment.

The spirit of God by himself is a discerner. We may not have the ability to detail the source and extent of error, without the gift, but we will detect the presence of error. Often, it results in an uneasiness in our spirit and we only know *"something just does not feel right."*

That brings us to the point where we must address an issue that is commonly raised. It is that *"Everyone who has the spirit of God has faith"*.

> *"Without faith it is impossible to please him: for he that cometh to God must believe that his is, and that he is a rewarder of them that diligently seek him."* (Hebrews 11:6).

However, the fact that we have faith is not one and the same as having the Gift of Faith. In the same way, having a measure of discernment resulting from us having the holy spirit, does not mean we have the gift of discernment.

This principle applies to other gifts such as healing etc. We might have prayed for healing for our self or for others and healing resulted.

That does not necessarily mean we have the gift of healing. Equally, even though we may not have the gift of healing does not mean we should not expect healing when we pray. Also, even though we may not have the gift of discernment, does not mean we are unable to discern a spiritual matter.

The difference is, when we have the gift, it becomes the principal means by which we serve to edify our local church and the area that others in the local church look to us for direction.

Another point that must be addressed is what happens when we receive the Holy Ghost. When we receive the holy-ghost, we all have the initial evidence of speaking in tongues. However, the initial evidence of speaking in tongues is not one and the same as the Gift of Tongues. This is important to note, as there is a fair bit of confusion on this subject that leads people to say: *"I have spoken in tongues so I have the Gift of Tongues"* or *"I have the holy-ghost but I don't speak in tongues, because I don't have the Gift of Tongues."*

These are all variations of a misunderstanding or failure to grasp the difference between the Gift of the Holy Ghost and the Gifts of the Spirit.

Let us return to the subject of discernment. There can be no denial that knowledge has increased in the earth. With the advent of the world wide web, complex information is readily available in real time in the palm of our hands. How many of us have diagnosed our own medical conditions through web MD.?

How many have done diagnostics on our car by watching YouTube video. How many have taught yourself to play a song or an instrument using YouTube video tutorials. I imagine the number is countless, no doubt. So yes, knowledge has increased.

However, discernment of Spirits is not to be confused or mistaken for educational or intellectual knowledge. God gives the gift of discernment even in the absence of intellectual knowledge. This supernatural knowledge is that which, by myself I cannot know or is unable to me. Stated another way, I cannot know what the spirit discerns by reading or study. This discerned knowledge is not knowable, except that it is revealed by the Spirit of God.

Intellectual knowledge is based on work by someone with expertise in a particular field of study. It follows rules, natural laws, as ordered by extensive research, study, observation, empirical data, tests, I could go on and on.

Scientists have derived laws that govern gravity, floatation, aerodynamics, electricity, relativity, statistics, psychology, economics and so on. We know these things because we spent time studying them.

We use statistical data to interpolate and extrapolate and make inferences. We determine best lines of fit. We predict behaviour and outcomes based on psychological profiles and models.

However, there is no study I can pursue to tell me what a particular brother or sister in the congregation did the previous night. I cannot study what an individual is praying for in their heart, or what they have fleeced God for. But, by the revelation of the spirit, I can discern that my brother is being swayed by an evil spirit and I can identify what that spirit is. This is revelation knowledge.

Revelation allows us to see into the spirit of another person and to discern that a particular thing is causing oppression and how to relieve them of that oppressive spirit. It can detect darkness and distinguish light. It is the means by which we are able to determine when one is walking in error. When faced with a dilemma, it enables us to make the right choice.

Sometimes, discerning is not just applied to spirits. It is simply supernatural ability. In discerning, it may be about doctrinal matters, it answers the question is there an error in what I am hearing?

Let us use the visible light spectrum to illustrate and illuminate this point. The visible light spectrum consists of the following colors: violet, indigo, blue, green, yellow, orange and red. The wavelength of lights reflecting from these colors can be seen by the naked eyes. However, lights with wavelengths outside this spectrum is not visible to the naked eye. Adjacent to violet, is ultra-violet at one end of the spectrum. At the other end of the spectrum adjacent to red, is Infra-red.

The fact that the eye cannot see beyond violet and red extremities of the spectrum, does not mean they do not exist. It simply means we need special enhancements to the naked eye to be able to detect this wavelength.

Like the visible spectrum, un-regenerated man (*man without the spirit of God*) cannot see the things that are spiritual. Without the gift of the spirit, we are limited to the full knowledge of spiritual things around us, and are literally blind to it. When our vision is enhanced by the Spiritual Gift of Discernment, suddenly we can see spiritually, what is going on around us.

Through the special lens of the spiritual gift, we can see outside the things that are invisible to the naked eye. In this example, the spiritual gift of Discernment is equivalent to the special glasses that must be worn by individuals to be able to see Ultra-violet and Infra-red rays.

Taking this further, it is similar to how an X-Ray, Ultra Sound, C-T Scan once completed, is able to show what is affecting my internal organs, even though I can't see it with my naked eye.

The Gift of Discernment subject's things to scrutiny, analysis and gives the diagnosis, even though I cannot tell by just looking on the outside.

Here are some points to consider as it relates to the operating this gift.

† Discernment is very helpful when we have to minister to others. It allows us to speak directly to the spirit that is present and may be causing an ailment or infirmity. Notice, Jesus cast out a deaf and dumb spirit out of a many they brought to him because he was dumb.

† Having discerned the cause of infirmity, Jesus spoke directly to the spirit and made him whole

† Pay close attention to who you share insights of what you have discerned with

† Don't become arrogant with the exercise of your gift. Always seek to edify people and glorify God

† Exercise the Gift of Love while you exercise this gift

† Be cautious, you can deliver the right message the wrong way and damage the life of a brother or sister

† Carefully choose when, where, why and how you use the gift

† Understanding Spiritual Warfare can be a useful tool and serve you well and enhance your ministry in this gift.

CHAPTER FIVE
# EVANGELISM

*"And he gave some, apostles; and some, prophets; and some, evangelists; and some, pastors and teachers."* (Ephesians 4:11).

### Gift Definition

## To be a messenger of the good news of the Gospel of Jesus Christ.

---

This word is derived from the Greek *euaggelistes* -meaning, preacher of the gospel (from eu – well, angelos – messenger, hence messenger of good).

This gift is listed in Ephesians 4:11 as one of the Five-fold Ministries. This elevates this gift as a resident means by which the carrier of this gift serves the body of Christ.

The Minister brings good news of Christ, essentially – the salvation message. So in general terms, this gift is used to advance the Gospel of Christ and bring conversion to others. Persons with this gift will look for opportunities to reach out to others, with the view and purpose to bring them to Christ.

Ideally, to exercise this gift well, one needs to be conscious of:

† Cross-Cultural Issues – how to share the gospel with others from non-western culture. How do you share the gospel with an agnostic? How would you approach the conversation about God with an atheist?

† Do you use the bible to show the existence of God to those who do not believe in the bible?

† You have to seek other means to appeal to those who are unbelievers and will challenge the basis of your belief. If the one to whom you are witnessing does not believe in your fundamental truths, then what? What about using the facts of nature? What about the laws of sowing & reaping? What about using your own life experiences and your own circumstances? What about your personal testimony? What about sharing a personal miracle? Or sharing a miracle you witnessed? The well-known secret is that the bible (the word of God) gives us the tools to use when ministering to those who do not believe in the bible. Here are some examples:

*"Because that which may be known of God is manifest in them; for God hath shewed it unto them. For the invisible things of him from the creation of the world are clearly seen, being understood by the things that are made, even his eternal power and Godhead; so that they are without excuse."* (Romans 1:19-20).

*"The heavens declare the glory of God and the firmament showeth his handiwork."* (Psalm 19:1).

So, we do have tools that empower us to reach say an atheist.

How do you reach an Atheist?

1. Don't be shocked by the fact they are atheist. Don't be phased (many Christians will end the conversation with this knowledge. But no, keep going)

2. Ask questions about their atheism. Is it really atheism or is it agnosticism?

3. Ask questions about their background. Don't be surprised if they were raised in church

4. Were they taught atheism or came to that conclusion? Who knows, there may be common ground. Paul found common ground with the worshippers in Athens who worshipped an unknown God

5. Maybe the atheist has an opinion of Christians, church or religion

6. Maybe the atheist has an opinion of Jesus (read about, or heard about)

7. Listen deeply for the real reason why. The real reason could be anger. It could be they came to that conclusion after loosing a loved one due to a lack of hope.

8. Try to form a connection relationally. Form a common bond. Atheists are real people, with real feelings. Resist the temptation to treat them as though they are lost or hopeless

9. Try to present the gospel as a love story, instead of trying to prove that God exists. Just share the story of the love of God

10. Even if you don't turn the atheist to Christ, you would have shared the gospel with them

In order to effectively minister in this Gifting, one needs to have tools suitable for cross-cultural purpose. To equip oneself to do so, I recommend that ministers understand Christian apologetics.

In summary, Apologetics is - defending against objection and knowing what other religions know and believe. It also includes knowing how to respond to questions asked of us, in relation to our belief.

Peter's instruction to the church is as follows:

> *"But sanctify the Lord God in your hearts: and be ready always to give an answer to every man that asketh you a reason of the hope that is in you with meekness and fear."* (I Peter 3:15).

In reality, sometimes the Evangelist has to reach across boundaries, borders, cultures and territories to reach others. This may require foregoing previously established protocols. As long as foregoing such protocols does not violate God-established scriptural principles, this may be ok. In other words, the need of evangelism may be more pressing, than maintaining a particular norm of protocol and procedure.

Having said that, those who operate in this gift must be aware of cultural norms and customs and strive to maintain them, as much as is possible.

To ensure this, there are some tools that we should have in our evangelism tool-kit that we can draw out. In past years, carpenters used hammers and nails in every fastening job. Today, carpenters use power tools and staples. An efficient carpenter is always looking for new, updated tools to help him perform his job efficiently and at a lower cost. In the same way, those exercising the Gift of Evangelism should be searching for new tools to help them become more efficient in their ministry. In the face of new and upcoming religions today, various sectors of people making up the society the Evangelist's challenge has never been greater.

Here are some questions that the Evangelist should seek answers to:

&dagger;  How do I present the Gospel to one who has never heard it?

&dagger;  How do I present Christ to one who is an Agnostic? A Skeptic?

&dagger;  How do I present the Gospel to my co-workers when there is a work-policy to refrain from religious discussions?

&dagger;  Am I even convinced there is one way to God?

&dagger;  What about all those other religions that exist?

&dagger;  What scriptural requirements are essential and which are optional?

&dagger;  Will I be able to present the gospel of Jesus without a bible? Without reference to the bible?

CHAPTER SIX

# EXHORTATION

*"Or he that exhorteth, on exhortation: he that giveth, let him do it with simplicity; he that ruleth, with diligence; he that sheweth mercy, with cheerfulness."* (Romans 12: 8).

### Gift Definition

**To come alongside another with words of encouragement, comfort, consolation, counsel to help them. Derived from the Greek *paraklesis* – calling to one's side.**

---

One of the most well-known passage of scripture that shows the paraclete is:

> *"And I will pray the father, and he shall give you another comforter that he may abide with you for ever. But the comforter, which is the Holy Ghost, whom the Father will send in my name, he shall teach you all things, and bring all things to your remembrance, whatsoever I have said unto you."*
> (St. John 14:16, 26).

John is the only writer that uses the word parakletos – rendered comforter

(St. John 14: 16, 26; 15:26; 16:7). In I John 2:1, the word *"Advocate"* is used, meaning one called to the side of another for help and counsel.

In the context of John's writing, the spirit is our paraclete or helper on earth, and Christ is the paraclete or helper in heaven.

The Gift of Exhortation is given by the Spirit to some in the body of Christ, to enable them to personify this work of the Spirit, to exhort, counsel, encourage others. During the time of his affliction, Job, from the Old Testament had a visit from his friends including Eliphaz to fill the role of counsellor in Job 16:2. Of course in Job's despair, he did not receive comfort from his friends.

The paraclete is foundational to understanding the Gift of Exhortation. It is to be understood as one who is called to the side of another to comfort them. It also provides words of encouragement, consolation or words of counsel.

By virtue of this role of the paraclete, the Gift of Exhortation is useful in situations other than a church setting. Often, it may be used to help in a witnessing situation, counselling a soul through a difficult personal problem or issue, such as a loss, major disappointment, financial crisis or health related problems.

In other cases, this gift may be used to help someone in their professional life, such as career choice, relocation or education decisions. Ministries that can benefit from the active application of this gift include Family Ministries, Singles Ministry, Follow-up Ministry and Youth Ministry.

Apostle Paul gave us glimpses of himself exercising the Gift of Exhortation in I Corinthians 7 as follows:

† Advice to married, verses 3-6

† Advice to unmarried, verses 7-9

† Advice concerning virgins, verses 25-28

† Advice to parents concerning marriageable age, verses 36-38

† Advice to Christian widows, verses 39-40s

Essentially, most of Paul's writing in the Epistles is a display of Exhortation. He does so in three distinct areas as follows:

**a. Doctrine**

**b. Instructions**

**c. Admonishing**

**Doctrine** – from the Greek didaskalia, is the act of teaching or that which is taught.

As it relates to the doctrine of Christ, it is the body of essential theological truths that define the message. It includes historical facts and is built around the life of Christ. Doctrine is indispensable to Christianity. New Testament scriptures repeatedly emphasizes the value and importance of sound doctrine and sound teachings:

*"If any man teach otherwise, and consent not to wholesome words, even the words of our Lord Jesus Christ, and to the doctrine which is according to godliness; He is proud, knowing nothing, but doting about questions and strifes of words, whereof cometh envy, strife, railings, evil surmisings."* (I Timothy 6:3).

*"Hold fast the form of sound words, which thou hast heard of me, in faith and love which is in Christ Jesus. That good thing which was committed unto thee keep by the Holy Ghost which dwelleth in us."* (II Timothy 1:13, 14).

The apostles encouraged believers to be faithful to that body of information they had heard and received in the beginning.

*"Holding fast the faithful word as he hath been taught, that he may be able by sound doctrine both to exhort and to convince the gainsayers."* (Titus 1:9).

*"Let that therefore abide in you, which ye have heard from the beginning. If that which ye have heard from the beginning shall remain in you, ye shall continue in the Son, and in the Father."* (I John 2:24).

*"But though we, or an angel from heaven, preach any other gospel unto you than that which we have preached unto you, let him be accursed."* (Galatians 1:8).

**Instructions -** This refers to detailed information indicating how something should be done.

This information must be based on sound doctrine. The instructions provided to the body of Christ has at its root the Inspired word of God, and its associated principles. Paul gave numerous instructions in his Epistles. Here are some examples of instructions he gave to Timothy:

† How to be a good minister – 4:6-11

† How to treat Elder Widows – 5:3-10

† How to tread church elders – 5:17-19

† Here are some examples of instructions he gave to Titus:

† How to tread the aged women – Titus 2:3

† What to teach young women – Titus 2:4-5

† What to teach young men – Titus 2:6-8

† How to treat servants – Titus 2:9-14

**Admonishing -** This refers to a warning, reprimand or sharp rebuke.

Here is an example from Paul's letter to the Thessalonians:

> *"And if any man obey not our word by this epistle, note that man,*
> *and have no company with him, that he may be ashamed. Yet*
> *count him not as an enemy, but admonish him as a brother."*
> (II Thessalonians 3:14-15).

Here is Jude's general admonishing in his epistle:

> *"..earnestly contend for the faith that was once delivered unto the*
> *saints."* (v.3).

Pastors are admonished to cleave to sound doctrine so thy could be good
ministers of the gospel (I Timothy 4:6).

Perhaps one of the greatest expressions and exercise of the Gift of Exhortation shown in scripture is seen in Barnabas.

> *"And Joses, who by the apostles was surnamed Barnabas, (which is, being interpreted, The son of consolation), a Levite, and of the country of Cyprus. Having land, sold it, and brought the money and laid it at the apostle's feet."* (Acts 4:36-37).

Barnabas, personified consolation. When the apostles in Jerusalem were afraid to receive the new convert Paul, Barnabas spoke on his behalf, and removed their apprehension.

On the report reaching Jerusalem that Christians of Cyprus and Cyrene had been proclaiming the gospel with great success to Greeks as well as to Jews at Antioch of Syria, the Church sent Barnabas and 'aided in the work'. Later, Barnabas accompanied Paul to the Church Council at Jerusalem. Barnabas spoke on that occasion to confirm that God had visited the Gentiles and had confirmed his work with signs and wonders. The report from Barnabas helped in the formulation of the Apostles directive that the Gentiles should not be required to observe the token of Circumcision. At the end of the Council, both Barnabas and Paul were commissioned to carry the decrees of the council to the churches in Syria and Asia Minor.

After further labors at Antioch, Paul proposed a second missionary journey. Barnabas desired to have with him his relative John Mark (Colossians 4:10). Paul objected, as John Mark had withdrawn from the work on the former tour. After sharp contention, the two (Paul and Barnabas) separated and went different ways. Barnabas and Mark sailed again to Cyprus, while Paul went on to Asia Minor.

Later in his epistle, Paul spoke in a cordial and respectful way of Barnabas

(I Corinthians 9:6; Galatians 2:1,9,13; Colossians 4:10) and yet more so of John Mark, about whom the quarrel arose (II Timothy 4:11).

Finally, to those who believe they have the Gift of Exhortation or those who would like to further educate themselves on this gift, you will find that literature on lay counselling, shepherding or teaching may to be particularly helpful.

# CHAPTER SEVEN

# FAITH

*"And there are diversities of operations, but it is the same God which worketh all in all. But the manifestation of the Spirit is given to ever man to profit withal. For to one is given by the spirit the word of wisdom, to another the word of knowledge by the same spirit. To another faith by the same Spirit, to another the gifts of healing by the same Spirit. To another the working of miracles; to another prophecy; to another discerning of spirits; to another diverse kinds of tongues; to another the interpretation of tongues":* (I Corinthians 12: 6-10).

## Gift Definition

**To be firmly persuaded of God's power and promises to accomplish his will and purpose and to display such a confidence in him and his word, that circumstances and obstacles do notshake that conviction.**

---

The faith which we will discuss in the next few pages is not to be confused with the Fruit of the Spirit (Galatians 5:22), which is a produced by the Holy Spirit and cultivated by the believer. That faith is more an expression of faithfulness.

Faith is a basic and essential elemental of salvation, and requirement for being a Christian. This is the conclusion of scripture:

> *"But without Faith it is impossible to please him, for he that cometh to God must believe that he is, and that he is a rewarder of them that diligently seek him."* (Hebrews 11:6).

The converse of the scripture is, that everyone who is a Christian, a believer, everyone who is filled with the Holy Spirit has faith. This supported by other scriptures:

> *"If you confess with your mouth and believe with your heart that God raised him from the dead, you shall be saved."* (Romans 10:9).

Faith is counter intuitive to human intelligence. Confidence in the work and ability of an individual is evidence based.

Faith requires that we show confidence and are assured of God's ability even when we do not see. The Gift of Faith is exercised in the face of evidence to the contrary.

Faith is not based on intellect, comprehension or human knowledge. Rather it is based on our knowledge of God and our confidence in him. The Gift of Faith steps outside of its own order and sphere.

There are different levels of faith that should be distinguished:

**Basic Faith** - Is that essential faith that all believers have, that is required for salvation. It is not to be confused with Gift of Faith. It encompasses:

**Belief** – deep passionate belief concerning the person and work of Christ. This is referenced as a creed – the doctrine we profess to believe.

**Trust** – confidence, unshaken confidence, assurance. Daniel and the Hebrew boys indicated their trust in God as follows:

> *"If it be so, our God whom we serve is able to deliver us from the burning fiery furnace, and he will deliver us out of thine hand, O king. But if not, be it know unto thee, O king, that we will not serve thy gods, nor worship the golden image which thou hast set up."* (Daniel 3:17-18).

**Obedience** – Unconditionally doing what God requires, without regard to the consequence.

> *"Why call ye me, Lord, Lord and do not the things which I say?"* (St. Luke 6:46).

## Great Faith

Over and above the exercise of basic faith, some within the body of Christ have understood that God has given power to act on his behalf in things concerning his Kingdom.

Two examples are provided in the new testament and are worth studying. Each drawing attention to aspects of what Faith is.

> *"And when Jesus was entered into Capernaum, there came unto him a centurion, beseeching him, and saying, Lord, my servant lieth at home sick of the palsy, grievously tormented.*
>
> *And Jesus saith unto him, I will come and heal him. The centurion answered and said, Lord, I am not worthy that thou shouldest come under my roof: but speak the word only, and my servant shall be healed.*

SPIRITUAL GIFTS

*For I am a man under authority, having soldiers under me: and I say to this man, Go, and he goeth; and to another, Come, and he cometh; and to my servant, Do this, and he doeth it. When Jesus heard it, he marvelled, and said to them that followed, Verily I say unto you, I have not found so great faith, no, not in Israel."* (St. Matthew 8:5-10).

In this example, the Centurion showed Great Faith, but of more importance, demonstrated an understanding of Authority. The Gift of Faith is an expression of exercise of spiritual authority. So, using the interaction between Jesus and the Centurion as a guide, we conclude that Faith is exercising 'Power of Attorney'. This Authority is putting into action Jesus' own words: *"All power is given unto me in heaven and in earth."*

In the second example, Jesus had an interaction with a Canaanite woman:

*"Then Jesus went thence, and departed into the coasts of Tyre and Sidon. And, behold a woman of Canaan came out of the same coasts, and cried unto him, saying, have mercy on me, O Lord, thou son of David; my daughter is grievously vexed with a devil. But he answered not a word.*

*And his disciples came and besought him, saying, Send her away; for she crieth after us. But he answered and said, I am not sent but unto the lost sheep of the house of Israel. Then came she and worshipped him, saying, Lord help me. But he answered and said, it is not meet to take the children's bread, and to cast it to dogs.*

*And she said, truth, Lord: yet the dogs eat of the crumbs which fall from their masters' table. Then Jesus answered and said unto her, O woman, great is thy faith: be it unto thee even as thou wilt.*

*And her daughter was made whole from that very hour.*"
(St. Matthew 15:21-28).

Here we are introduced to a Gentile woman, making a request of Jesus for what she was not legally entitled. Not only was she not legally entitled to it, the time was not yet come for the granting of such request. This interaction with Jesus and her request was within the Dispensation of the Law.

The Dispensation of Grace would not commence until after the death of Christ on the cross. So, in essence, she asked for something which was somewhat out of 'order'. What she asked for would only become due during the dispensation of Grace.

With that in mind, she engaged Jesus in a legal argument. The woman acknowledged her position as undeserving and without legal covenant rights to the children's (*Jews*) bread, and yet she used what was her knowledge concerning dogs as grounds for further claim for healing. Even dogs have some rights – rights to the crumbs that the master throws away and would give to them.

Children have enough bread and to spare, so she claimed the scraps for her daughter. She won her case. Christ could not turn down such faith.

These two interactions are the only instances in scripture where Christ referred to Great Faith. The implication of these two references is that faith, when exercised, has the ability to move God even beyond boundaries that existed previously. In one instance, the Centurion showed how to exercise the authority (Greek: exousia) that Christ gives to the church, while in the other instance it shows how the woman got Christ to act out of turn in relation to keeping with his Dispensational plan. It shows faith can get God's attention, even when God, by established order should not act. How powerful is this tool in the hand of the believer!

# The operation of the Gift of Faith

Faith does not exist independently; neither does the Gift of Faith operate without action. For this reason, this gift typically operates as a compliment with other gifts, such as the gifts of healing or miracles. Here are some examples of the Gift in operation:

&#10014; Gift of Faith operated in the raising of Lazarus. Bound in grave-clothes, the decomposed dead body of Lazarus was re-suscitated when Jesus Called in a loud voice *'Lazarus, come forth'* (St. Luke 11:43)

&#10014; The Gift of Faith was in operation in the case of the fig-tree. In that encounter, Jesus said *'Let no fruit grow on thee henceforward for ever. And presently the fig tree withered away'*. (St. Matthew 21:19).

&#10014; The Gift of Faith is in operation in the story of Ananias and Sapphira, who both lied to the Holy Spirit. *'Then Peter said unto her, how is it that ye have agreed together to tempt the Spirit of the Lord? Behold, the feet of them which have buried thy husband are at the door and shall carry thee out. Then fell she down straightway at his feet, and yielded up the ghost: and the young men came in, and found her dead, and, carrying her forth, buried her by her husband'*. (Acts 5:9-10).

In these examples of the Operation of the Gift of Faith, there is clearly the Gift of Miracles in operation as well.

CHAPTER EIGHT
# GIVING

*"Having then gifts differing according to the grace that is given to us, whether prophecy, let us prophesy according to the proportion of faith; Or ministry, let us wait on our ministering: or he that teacheth, on teaching; Or he that exhorteth, on exhortation: he that giveth, let him do it with simplicity; he that ruleth, with diligence; he that sheweth mercy, with cheerfulness."*
(Romans 12:6-8).

### Gift Definition

**To share what material resource you have, liberally and with cheerfulness without thought or expectation of return.**

---

The Gift of Giving is one of a group that are referred to as *"Serving Types"* of Spiritual Gifts, these are: **Giving, Helps, Hospitality and Mercy.**

There are some common themes that generally run through all of the Serving Gifts. On the other hand, there are some unique distinctions that should be observed as follows:

**The Gift of Giving** is a "*resource oriented*" gift, which generally provides funds or other material needed.

**The Gift of Helps** is a "*staff oriented*" gift, and generally provides assistance so others can do their job effectively.

**The Gift of Hospitality** is a "*relationship oriented*" gift, and generally makes people feel welcomed and comfortable.

**The Gift of Mercy** is a "*compassion oriented*" gift, and generally helps in comforting, restoring and caring for people who may have fallen out of good standing with another, or with the church.

At the core of those who operate in the gift of giving is *benevolence*. Benevolence is an act of kindness or an inclination to be kind. It is what drives an individual to volunteer their time to help in soup kitchens, provide free tutor to struggling students, drive seniors to medical appointments, or visit shut-ins to help them clean up their homes. Scriptures are replete with teachings and principles based on benevolent giving.

Giving in its simplest form has Love at its root. Giving is motivated by love. When giving is generated by love, there is no expectation to receive anything in return. For example, when a parent gives tirelessly to their children; by waking up in the middle of the night to soothe a crying toddler, to calm them after a bad dream or make their favourite snack, there is no expectation to receive a reward, payment or even any thing in return. That is just out of love. Love is a sufficient motivator for such actions.

The principle of giving originates from God.

> "*For God so loved the world that he gave his only begotten son that whosoever believeth on him should not perish but have everlasting life.*" (St. John 3:16).

From this and other scriptures, we conclude there is a direct relationship between love and giving. Love is an action word. Where there is love there is an action to show what that love does or accomplishes. Love expresses itself through action, usually giving.

Here are examples showing how love is always associated with giving.

> *"Greater love hath no man than this, that a man laid down (gave) his life for his friend."* (St. John 15:13).

> *"But Love ye your enemies, and do good, and lend, hoping for nothing again; and your reward shall be great, and ye shall be the children of the highest: for he is kind unto the unthankful and to the evil."* (St. Luke 6:35).

> *"Husbands, love your wives, even as Christ also loved the church, and gave himself for it;"* (Ephesians 5:25).

> *"But whoso hath this world's goods, and seeth his brother have need, and shutteth up his bowels of compassion from him, how dwelleth the love of God in him?"* (I John 3:17).

> *"My little children, let us not love in word, neither in tongue; but is deed and in truth."* (I John 3:18).

So, in essence, everyone who is born of God, and loves his brother has the natural inclination to give. Conversely, if we do not give, it shows we do not love.

Most persons in Christendom can embrace giving but based on conditions, such as:

† They know the person to whom they give (they identify with the person)

† They have the wherewithal to give (there is no cost or low cost)

† The person to whom they give is deserving of the gift

But, what if these conditions are not present. If instead, the opposite is true, what drives giving in those circumstances? This is where the Gift of Giving comes in. This gift will keep giving even in the following circumstances:

† The object of giving is unknown

† Giving is purely out of sacrifice

† The person requiring the gift is deemed unworthy and undeserving

Then, in these instances, giving is motivated by love, compassion, mercy, benevolence or helps.

Scriptures relating instances of blessings bestowed on those that gave sacrificially to motivate others who are not so inclined. Some examples are provided here as follow:

† The widow of Zarephath – I Kings 17:1-14

† The widow and Jesus at the temple – St. Mark 12:41-44

† Abraham – Genesis 22:16-16

† David – II Samuel 254:24

Should we conclude that the gift of giving is **Love**?

CHAPTER NINE

# HEALING

*"To another faith by the same Spirit; to another the gifts of
healing by the same Spirit."*

*"And God hath set some in the church, first apostles, secondarily
prophets, thirdly teachers, after that miracles, then gifts of
healings, helps, governments, diversities of tongues."*
(I Corinthians 12:9, 28).

### Gift Definition

### To be used as a means through which God makes People whole, whether physically, emotionally, mentally or spiritually.

Firstly, we should note carefully that the gift described in verse 9 is a plurality of gifts. The meaning and application of this plurality is to be understood in the same way that there are various medical practitioners that we visit, depending on our medical complaint. There are cardiologists, urologists, oncologists, Podiatrists, Gynecologists, etc. They all help with wellness of the body, but they specialize in different things. We could add to the list, Psychologists, and Psychiatrists, to address non-physical related issues. In the same way, we can understand that God administer the Gift of Healing within the Church, where the one operating in the Gift, may minister predominantly to people in the body with cancer. God may use another individual to minster to those who have mental problems and so on.

In another sense, we could look at the gifts of healing as one gift may relate to the physiological man – the normal functions of the man and his body. Another gift of healing could be directed towards the mental health of the man – involving the cognitive thinking and processing of information, related to brain function. Still, another gift could be directed toward the emotional health – involving one's ability to express their emotion (inner feeling) in an appropriate way.

Regarding the **Gifts of Healing**, this is related to the other Power Gifts, which are: **Gift of Faith** and **Gift of Miracles**.

No one person has a monopoly on every sort of healing. Also, there will be many times, an individual who operates in the Gift of Healing may not be able to heal a particular sickness that has been presented to them.

Apostle Paul, who no doubt operated in this gift, healed:

    ✝   A crippled man at Lystra – Acts14:10

    ✝   Many people at Ephesus – Acts 19:12

    ✝   A demoniac girl at Philippi – Acts 16:18

    ✝   Eutycus, after he fell from a Window – Acts 20:9-10

However, Paul did not heal on several occasions as follows:

    ✝   Himself from the thorn in his flesh – II Corinthians 12:8-9

† Ailment when he preached in Galatia – Galatians 4:13-14

† Timothy from stomach ailment – I Timothy 5:23

† Epaphroditus from life threatening sickness – Philippians 2:26-27

† Trophius whom he "left ill at melitus" II Timothy 4:20.

We should note it is the spirit who apportions the gifts to each one individually as he pleases.

Healing is a great way to draw others to God. Those who are healed are expected to respond to say thanks, like the ten lepers in Luke 17: 15-19. By God's grace, physical healing often results in spiritual healing. In fact, physical healing has often served as a gateway to spiritual healing. Often, people who have experienced healing will be open and receptive to receiving the message of salvation.

One of the attributes of those who possess The Gift of Healing is they also possess compassion and empathy towards the sick. This is directly related to the spirit of God, and is patterned after Jesus Christ.

> *"And when the Lord saw her, he had compassion on her and said unto her. Weep not."* (St. Luke 7:13).

> *"Then Jesus called his disciples unto him, and said, I have compassion on the multitude, because they continue with me now three days, and have nothing to eat, and I will not send them away fasting, lest they faint in the way."* (St. Matthew 15:32).

There are three essential elements that must be present for effectively operating in this gift. These are: **Faith, Prayer and Counselling**.

**Faith** has been covered independently in chapter 7 of this book, so I will briefly address Prayer because of its importance to all the *Power Gifts*.

# Prayer

Prayer as a ministry, can take many forms. It can be personal, with a prayer partner, or corporate group such as the church. Regardless of the format, effective praying requires specific ingredients as follows:

- Establish and maintain a personal relationship with God – James 5:16

- Based on the right purpose and perspective – Prayer is effective when we pray for the will of God

- Develop a passion for praying

- View prayer as a priority, not an afterthought, or for convenience

- Adhere to biblical principles when praying

- Know that prayer was instituted by God, so we can communicate with him

- Approach God on his terms, not on ours

- Pray back God's words to him

Here is a resource that I found to help you to Pray the Psalms

1. When you want to praise God – Psalms 92:1-2, 100, 150

2. When times are hard – 138:7,8: 94:17-19: 18:1-2

3. When you want God's protection – 27:4-8; 91:1-16

4. When you are tempted to retaliate – 37:7-9

5. When you want God's guidance – 32:8: 27:1,14

Here are some recommended readings on improving one's prayer life:

> *"The Prayer of Jabez"* – Bruce Wilkinson
> *"Prayer for Amateurs"* – Jane Holloway, and
> *"Too Busy not to Pray"* – Bill Hybels

Here are some of the principles that govern the gifts of Healing:

† Healing proceeds from God, and is available through the atoning work of Jesus Christ

† Although the gifts of Faith and Miracles extend beyond the realm of Healing, they are often integrated into this gift

† This gift operates in conjunction with other gifts (faith, miracles, word of knowledge)

† Fundamental to this gift is the principle on which Jesus operated, that the Son can do nothing by himself; which conveys that the work of healing is only accomplished through the Spirit of God

The purpose of Healing can be summarized for brevity as follows:

- ✝ To contribute to the wholeness of an individual

- ✝ To alleviate physical suffering

- ✝ To cleanse the soul

- ✝ To release the emotions

- ✝ To edify believers to be aware of the presence and ministry of the Holy Spirit

- ✝ To be a sign to believers that the Kingdom has come

- ✝ To bring Glory to God

- ✝ That the work of God might be manifested

Those who administer healing to others are aware that this ministry is accomplished by engaging in Spiritual Warfare. Many times, those who need healing are being oppressed by demonic forces, as sickness is often the domain of the devil. "How God anointed Jesus of Nazareth with the Holy Ghost and with power: who went about doing good, and healing all that were oppressed of the devil; for God was with him." (Acts 10:38).

- ✝ Those involved in the Healing Ministry have experienced some level of spiritual conflict

- ✝ The enemy attacks both before, during and after a healing ministry

- ✝ An individual may be anointed for different conditions on different occasions

✝ Some may develop faith for one area of healing, and not for another

✝ It is not uncommon for one to be given a word of wisdom, word of knowledge or prophecy for the person being healed

On the subject of physical healing, we are more concerned about illness caused by organic or chemical factors within the body that affects the body. This may also refer to functional disorders, such as PH balance, acid reflux, deterioration of cells, tumors, malfunction of organs etc.

Once physical healing takes place, there is an abatement of symptoms or absolute cure. The abatement may begin immediately and occurs gradually, or the healing can be instantaneous. Naaman the Leper – II Kings 5:1-15, is an example of a disease emanating from an organ disorder (organic). Scriptures does not say his leprosy was a result of sin or past evil.

In contrast to physical healing, Healing of the Spirit affects all other areas of an individual's life and personality. Healing of the Spirit is the renewal and restoration of a person's spiritual life. A renewal of his or her relationship with God.

Finally, here are some guidelines that those who operate in the Gift of Healing should bear in mind:

1. Invite the Holy Spirit and encourage the person being prayed for to welcome him

2. Watch for the manifestation of the Spirit of God upon the person's body and bless what God is doing

3. Be in tune with the Spirit to discern the root cause of the sickness. Lay hands on affected area if appropriate, if not appropriate, let them lay their own hands there

4. Listen to the Spirit of God for specific instructions or words of knowledge, which will contribute to the release of healing

5. Quiet the person if he/she is too emotional and unable to focus

6. Break the power of doubt, unbelief, fear etc., in the name of Jesus Christ

7. Speak to the condition and tell it to go, or be healed. Jesus said, we must speak to mountains – this is a Jewish metaphor for difficulty

8. Be familiar with scripture passages where the healing ministry is effective. Example, Jesus rebuked the fever in Peter's mother-in-law

# CHAPTER TEN
# HOSPITALITY

*"Use hospitality one to another without grudging. As every man hath received the gift, even so minister the same one to another, as good stewards of the manifold grace of God." (I Peter 4:9-10).*

## Gift Definition

**To warmly welcome people, even strangers, into one's home or church as a means of serving their needs.**

---

This gift originates from the Greek *Philoxenos*; philos – love, xenos – stranger. Not surprisingly, this gift is literally bestowed upon those who love strangers. Apostle Paul instructs Titus as follows:

*"For a bishop must be blameless, as the steward of God; not self willed, not soon angry, not given to wine, no striker, nor given to filthy lucre, But a lover of hospitality, a lover of good men, sober, just holy, temperate." (Titus 1:7-8).*

Also to Timothy Paul warns as follows:

> *"A bishop then must be blameless, the husband of one wife, vigilant, sober, of good behaviour, given to hospitality, apt to teach."* (I Timothy 3:2).

A significant component of the Gift of Hospitality involves visitations. This includes visiting those who need encouragement, comfort or generally someone that needs a reminder they are not forgotten. This group includes:

- Elderly persons, especially those living alone and may be lonely

- People who are sick, especially those in care homes

- People who are hospitalized

- The Bereaved, those suffering from loss of a loved-one

- People who are incarcerated

- The homeless or those in shelters

- People whose life is in crisis – family, health, mental etc.

Here are some things to consider during visits to the above listed persons:

- Do more listening than talking

- Exercise wisdom and sensitivity in what you say

- Be respectful and understanding. You are there for them

- Don't be afraid to touch. Yes, it may be awkward but necessary

- Don't be surprised to see living conditions that may be less than you are accustomed

- Offer prayer before you leave

- Leave something as a reminder of your visit – card, flower, basket or fruit, food, cash, token etc.

- The scriptures are a great resource for use to help to bring comfort

CHAPTER ELEVEN

# MIRACLES

*"To another the working of miracles; to another prophecy, to another discerning of spirits; to another divers kinds of tongues; to another the interpretation of tongues:"*

*"And God hath set some in the church, first apostles, secondarily prophets, thirdly teachers, after that miracles, then gifts of healings, helps, governments, diversities of tongues."*
(I Corinthians 12:9, 28).

## Gift Definition

**To be enabled by God to perform mighty deeds, which witnesses acknowledge to be of supernatural origin and means.**

---

A miracle is a supernatural act. A suspension of the accustomed order. An intervention in the course of nature as it is normally understood.

Jesus performed miracles primarily out of compassion, both to meet human needs and for practical purposes. He walked on water to comfort his disciples. He fed the multitudes because food was unavailable. He turned water into wine to solve a crisis at a wedding.

It is difficult to distinguish between healing and miracles; however, we can apply the following rule:

a.  Healing includes acts of power that produce an abatement or a cure in the living body

b.  Other events that are miraculous manifestations beyond healings are plain miracles.

Similar acts, example: Signs and Wonders are included in God's program for extending the Kingdom of God in the earth. The preaching of the Kingdom is affirmed by manifestations of God's power which would serve as signs and wonders to the world. Miracles vindicate the name of Jesus and the Gospel. It causes those who witness them to reflect.

Some examples of Miracles can be summarized as:

a.  Israel escaped bondage in Egypt as a type of salvation. (Psalm 136:10-22)

b.  Provide water to quench Israel's thirst to Meet needs (Exodus 17, Mark 6:13, 30-44)

c.  Smite Egypt with plagues to Carry out diving judgment and discipline (Exodus 7-11)

d.  Smote Elymas with blindness to confirm the preached word - Acts 13:11-12

e.  Deliverance from unavoidable danger – Matthew 8:24-26, Acts 12:4-11

f.   Raise the Dead to demonstrate power over death – St. John 11:38-44

g.   Display God's power and magnificence – Psalm 145:3-7

## Guidelines on how the Gift of Miracles operates:

Firstly, no one can claim with certainty to know just how God works. He is sovereign, and rules by his own power and at his own good pleasure. He works however he wills. Regardless of who we are, we cannot demand a miracle from God. Instead we can use our God-given authority to command a miracle, wrought by the power of God.

There are some common themes which accompany miracles that we can highlight as follows:

- Deep compassion, or anger John 11:33-38, Matthew 9:36, Mark 3:5

- An accompanying Gift of Faith – An absolute conviction this this is God's will now.  Mark 10:46-52

- The person exercising the Gift of Miracle speaks the word or perform the act (or does both) which effects the miracle – Mark 7:33-35

# CHAPTER TWELVE
# PASTORS

*"And he gave some, apostles; and some, prophets, and some, evangelists; and some, pastors and teachers."* (Ephesians 4:11).

## Gift Definition

## To be responsible for spiritually caring, protecting, guiding and feeding a group of believers entrusted to one's care.

---

Two words have been used to identify the pastor. *Raah*, in the Old Testament and *Poimen*, in the New Testament. In both instances the overwhelming meaning is to feed a flock, to tend, to pasture. Interestingly, the word pastor has consistently been used synonymously with the Shepherd in scripture. So, in order to properly define the role of the pastor we will look closely at the shepherd.

There are three types of shepherds that have been identified in the Old Testament:

1. **Nomad Shepherds**
2. **Wealthy Sheep Owner**
3. **Settled Shepherd**

**The Nomad shepherd** owned flocks and herds.  He dwelt in tents, and moved from place to place to find pasture for their cattle. Here are some examples:

> *"And Adah bare Jabal: he was he father of such as dwell in tents, and of such as have cattle."* Genesis 4:20.

> *"And Abram was very rich in cattle, in silver, and in gold.  And he went on his journeys from the south even to Bethel, unto the place where his tent had been at the beginning, between Bethel and Hai: unto the place of he altar, which he had make there at first: and there Abram called on the name of the Lord."* (Genesis 13: 2-4).

**The Wealthy Sheep Owner** were those who dwelt in towns, while their flocks were driven from pasture to pasture by their servants.

Here are some examples:

> *"And there was a man in Maon, whose possessions were in Carmel, and the man was very great, and he had three thousand sheep, and a thousand goats: and he was shearing his sheep in Carmel.... And now I have heard that thou hast shearers: now thy shepherds which were with us, we hurt them not, neither was there ought missing unto them, all the while they were in Carmel...*

> *They were a wall unto us both by night and day, all the while we were with them keeping the sheep"* (I Samuel 25: 2-17).

> *"And his brethren went to feed their father's flock in Schechem. And Israel said unto Joseph, do not thy brethren feed the flock in Schechem? Come, and I will send thee unto them.  And he said to him, here am I.....And a certain man found him, and,*

*behold, he was wandering in the field: and the man asked him saying, What seekest thou? And he said, I seek my brethren: tell me, I pray thee, where they feed their flocks. And the man said, they are departed hence; for I heard them say, let us go to Dothan. And joseph went after his brethren, and found them in Dothan."* (Genesis 37:12-17).

**The settled Shepherd** led the flock from the permanent fold to the pasture in the morning and in the evening brought it home again. Jesus Christ described himself as this kind of shepherd:

> *"Verily, verily, I say unto you, he that entereth not by the door into the sheepfold, but climbeth up some other way, the same is a thief and a robber. But he that entereth in by the door is the shepherd of the sheep. To him the porter openeth; and the sheep hear his voice: and he calleth his own sheep by name, and leadeth them out. And when he putteth forth is own sheep, he goeth before them, and the sheep follow him: for they know his voice."* (St. John 10:1-4).

Take careful note that the shepherd is responsible to the owner for any loss of sheep.

> *"That which was torn of beasts I brought not unto thee; I bare the loss of it, of my hand didst thou require it, whether stolen by day, or stolen by night."* (Genesis 31:39).

The Mosaic Law relieved him from responsibility if he could prove that the loss was not due to his neglect.

> *"If a man delivers unto his neighbor an ass, or an ox, or a sheep, or any beast, to keep; and it die, or be hurt, or driven away, no man seeing it. Then shall an oath of the Lord be between them both, that he hath not put his hand unto his neighbor's goods; and*

*he shall not make it good. And if it be stolen from him, he shall make restitution unto the owner thereof. If it be torn in pieces, then let him bring it for witness, and he shall not make good that which was torn."* (Exodus 22:10-13).

The implication of this scripture is there is burden of responsibility that every pastor has. Literally, he has to give an account for all the flock over which he oversees.

## Duties of the Pastor

The scriptures have provided an abundance of references on the importance of the pastor, including the consequence of the pastor's failure. The overwhelming principal duty of the pastor is to feed the church.

*"And I will give you Pastors according to my Heart, which shall feed you with knowledge and understanding."* (Jeremiah 3:15).

*"For the Pastors are become brutish (rough, unpleasant, violent) and have not sough the Lord, therefore they shall not prosper."* (Jeremiah 10:21)

*"Many Pastor's have destroyed my vineyard, they have trodden my portion under foot, they have made my pleasant portion a desolate wilderness."* (Jeremiah 12:10).

Pastors must be aware of the impending judgment that awaits them if they err.

*"Woe be unto the Pastors that destroy and scatter the sheep of my pasture! saith the Lord. Therefore, thus saith the Lord God of Israel against the Pastors that feed my people; Ye have scattered my flock, and driven them away, and have not visited them:*

*behold, I will visit upon you the evil of your doings, saith the Lord."*
(Jeremiah 23:1-2).

To help to clarify the severity of the pronouncement against Pastors who fail in their duty, look at the meaning of woe. This word is derived from a Hebrew word which has the same meaning of a *'primary exclamation of grief'*. Literally, *Oh No!* It speaks of impending doom.

It is the exclamation of an onlooker who has witnessed the result of God's executed judgment. The fact that God reserves woe for Pastors who fail in their duty is a frightening proposition. Everyone who operates in the Office of the Pastor should take careful note.

The pastor has one of the most unique roles in the functioning of the Church. His role is identical to the role of a shepherd in ensuring the growth, survival and development of the sheep. The shepherd must take the sheep to pasture so they can be fed. It is the shepherd's duty to find fresh pasture, when the existing pastures are over-grazed. Not only must the shepherd ensure the flock is fed, he is responsible for the overall health of the sheep. If a particular sheep needs specific attention, he must attend to that need. It may even be necessary to personally carry that sheep in his hand, to ensure that sheep is cared for. Bearing in mind the great responsibility that rests on the shoulders of the Pastor and the uniqueness of his duties, there is no doubt those who minister in this office needs special qualifications. Here is a list of the qualifications for the office of the Pastor outlined in the book of Jeremiah;

✝ To be men after God's own heart.

> *"And I will give you pastors according to mine heart, which shall feed you with knowledge and understanding."* (Jeremiah 3:15).

✝ They feed the flock with Knowledge.

*"And I will set up shepherds over them which shall feed them and they shall fear no more nor be dismayed, neither shall they be lacking saith the Lord."* (Jeremiah 23:4).

✝ They know and teach God's Law.

*"The Priests said not, where is the Lord? And they that handle the law knew me not: the pastors also transgressed against me, and the prophets prophesied by Baal, and walked after things that do not profit."* (Jeremiah 2:8).

✝ They must be sensitive and reasonable and seek after God.

*"For the Pastors are become brutish, and have not sought the Lord: therefore, they shall not prosper, and all their flocks shall be scattered."* (10:21)

✝ They must protect and nourish the vineyard.

*"Many pastors have destroyed my vineyard, they have trodden my portion under foot, they have made my pleasant portion a desolate wilderness."* (12:10)

✝ They must protect and gather the sheep.

*"Woe be unto the pastors that destroy and scatter the sheep of my pasture saith the Lord."* (23:1)

✝ They must visit the sheep.

*"Therefore thus saith the Lord God of Israel against the pastors that feed my people; Ye have scattered my flock, and driven them*

*away, and have not visited them: behold, I will visit upon you the evil of your doings, saith the Lord."* (23:2)

✝ They must comfort the sheep in fear.

*"And I will set up shepherds over you hem which shall feed them: and they shall fear no more, nor be dismayed, neither shall they be lacking, saith the Lord."* (23:4

✝ They must supply the need of the sheep

✝ They must be morally clean (referring to them as being prophets in this context).

*"I have seen also in the prophets of Jerusalem an horrible thing: they commit adultery, and walk in lies: they strengthen also the hands of evildoers, that none doth return from his wickedness; they are all of them unto me as Sodom, and the inhabitants thereof as Gomorrah."* (23:14)

✝ They speak for God, not self.

*"Thus saith the Lord of Hosts, hearken not unto the words of the prophets that prophesy unto you: they make you vain: they speak a vision of their own heart, and not of the mouth of the Lord."* (23:16)

✝ They stand in God's counsel.

*"But if they had stood in my counsel, and had caused my people to hear my words, then they should have turned them from the evil of their doings."* (23:22)

† They must be free from deceit.

*"How long shall this be in the heart of he prophets that prophesy lies? Yea, they are prophets of the deceit of their own heart."* (23:26)

† They will cause people to remember God

*"Which think to cause my people to forget my name by their dreams which they tell every man to his neighbour, as their fathers have forgotten my name for Baal."* (23:27)

† They speak God's words faithfully (23:27).

Here are seven (7) guidelines to note the marks of a good pastor.

1.  Personal knowledge: no stranger to God or the gospel experiences

2.  Diving Call: not from greed, personal ambition, respect, honor self -interest, or love of ease

3.  Consecrated motives: God's will and glory, salvation of lost souls, and best interests of the church and all men

4.  Divine anointing: not human education, wisdom and effort only, but divine leading and help

5.  Personal Interest: acquaintance with his flock, private and public instruction, and helpfulness in all problems

6.  Good example: lead, not drive, feed, not destroy; and live what is preached

7.  Divine success: be zealous and fearless to protect, heal, preserve, increase, visit and sacrifice for the flock

Perhaps, the best way to summarize the role, responsibility and work of the Pastor is to repeat Paul's address to the Ephesian Elders: -

> *"Take heed therefore unto yourselves, and to all the flock, over the which   the Holy Ghost hath made you overseers, to feed the church of God, which he hath purchased with his own blood."* (Acts 20:28).

# CHAPTER THIRTEEN

# PROPHECY

*"Having then gifts differing according to the grace that is given to us, whether prophecy, let us prophesy according to the proportion of faith"* (Romans 12:6).

*"To another the working of miracles; to another prophecy; to another discerning of spirits; to another divers kinds of tongues; to another the interpretation of tongues"* (I Corinthians 12:10).

*"And he gave some, apostles; and some, prophets; and some, evangelists; and some, pastors and teachers."* (Ephesians 4:11).

## Gift Definition

### To speak forth the message of God or the message from God.

From the Greek *prophetes*: the forth-telling of the will of God: (Pro- forth, phemi – to speak).

Interestingly, this word is used as a Teacher or an interpreter of the will of God. In instances, it refers to a person who foretells events, as well as a person who advocates and speaks for the cause of God.

In the Greek context, it speaks of a person who recognizes the heart of God in a particular situation and expresses that to others.

Prophecy is declaring the message of God, either speaking directly or declaring the message for God. It is not a skill to be learned or studied. It is not based on aptitude or talent. It is speaking the words of the spirit related to a specific situation. The message ceases when the word given by the spirit ceases.

Let us look briefly at prophecy in the old testament in comparison to the new testament. We know that God spoke unto the fathers by the prophets, but in these last days he speaks by the Spirit. We note that the old testament prophets were appointed by God and served as checks and balance to the political power and authority of the kings.

In fact, we understand that the governance of Israel was accomplished through three branches. The Prophet, Priest and King. Under this system, the King was the Political ruler, the Priest the Spiritual leader with responsibility to show the people how to worship, and lead in matters of how to approach God through the tabernacle. The Prophet provided Godly guidance to the King and served as the voice of God including giving direction in war, and ensuring that justice and fairness is meted out to the people. All three branches were set up to work together to ensure there was accountability in the Monarchy that commenced in Israel at the end of the theocracy. It is interesting to note that the North American system of government is modelled after the system that God instituted in Israel. Under the North American system there is an Executive, Legislative and Judiciary branch co-existing independently and for the most part harmoniously. The Legislative and Judicial branch has the constitutional responsibility to ensure there are checks and balances in place on the Executive Branch so power and privilege is not abused. This is done by making laws to set the framework within which the Government operates and enforcing these laws when the government fails to do so.

In a similar way, the old testament prophets served as a constraint on the kings of Israel, and brought them back in line, when they erred. The story of the prophet Nathan and how he confronted king David regarding Uriah's wife is an example of this interplay. Similarly, Samuel the prophet, confronted King Saul regarding his conduct following God's command that he utterly destroy the Amalekites.

Being a prophet was a serious office in God's government of Israel. Admittedly, God's plan for governing Israel was always that he was their King. However, once it became clear they wanted to have a king of their own (rejected God's theocratic government), God set the office of the prophet in place. So crucial was the role of the prophet, that God enshrined the duty, role and seriousness of the prophet in his Laws. Because the prophet spoke for God, there was no room for error.

> *"And he said, hear now my words: If there be a prophet among you, I the Lord will make myself known unto him in a vision, and will speak unto him in a dream."* (Numbers 12:6).

> *"But the prophet which shall presume to speak a word in my name, which I have not commanded him to speak, or that shall speak in the name of other gods, even that prophet shall die."* (Deuteronomy 18:20).

> *"When a prophet speaketh in the name of the Lord, if the thing follow not, nor come to pass, that is the thing which the Lord hath not spoken, but the prophet hath spoken it presumptuously, thou shall not be afraid of him."* (Deuteronomy 18:22).

While the Old Testament prophets' ministries was essentially foretelling events, and being God's representative of the people to the King, New Testament prophets had a distinct change in character.

New Testament prophecy became more forth telling. Joel in his prophecy did notify that:

> "*And it shall come to pass afterward, that I will pour out my Spirit upon all flesh; and your sons and daughters shall prophesy.*" (Joel 2: 28).

The essential difference between the Old Testament and the New testament is that the Spirit of God overshadowed the Old Testament Prophets and moved upon them, while the Spirit indwells the Church in the New Testament. Given that the Holy Spirit now indwells the believers in the New Testament, there is not the same need for the voice of the prophet to remind the nations of God's direction as before. Instead of the prophet being the only voice of God in the earth, the prophetic office now serves to equip the body of Christ and bring it to perfection.

Prophecy in a general sense covers two areas: forthtelling and foretelling:

a. Forthtelling, such as preaching, teaching and evangelism, which could be through speaking, writing, drama and music, etc. A prophet may also be a person with a special burden for social justice (like Amos) who identifies areas in need of reform and who is emboldened to denounce the forces or sources of the evil. Such forthtelling usually emanates from and appeals to both the intellect and compassion of man.

b. Foretelling some events of the future such as John did broadly in the book of Revelation or Agabus did specifically and personally in the book of Acts (21:10,11).

The gift of prophecy is not confined to recognized prophets, but is more widely distributed in the church in fulfillment of Joel 2:28. So we read the following:

*"For you can all prophesy in turn"* (I Corinthians 14:31).

Briefly, let us address the question of the difference between the Gift of Prophecy and the Ministry of the Prophet. Though all can prophesy, by virtue of the Holy Spirit's anointing, not all are prophets. Though all can 'manifest' the gift of prophecy, only some are 'appointed' to the ministry of a prophet (I Corinthians 12: 7, 28,29; 14:29-33). Notice Agabus arrived at Caesarea to meet Paul, who was lodging with Philip the evangelist and his four daughters. Although these four girls had the gift of prophecy, Agabus had the Ministry of a prophet (named and featured in the book of acts). It was Agabus, not one of the four girls, who was entrusted with a major directive prophecy for Paul (Acts 21:8-11).

In I Corinthians 14, Paul encourages everyone to pursue the gift of prophecy. Based on this text, here are some of the ways the Gift of Prophecy serves the Church:

† Edification – Building up of the Church V3

† Encouragement & Instruction – v 31

† Exhortation – Admonishing and Warning v 3, Acts 21: 10-11

† Comfort – v3

† Conviction of Saints – Believers, Unbelievers can be brought to greater understanding of faith v 24-25

† Impartation – releasing Timothy through a Prophetic message – I Timothy 4:14

Prophecy is helpful to the body in a number of ways as follows:

1. Strengthen the body of Christ – Gird up

2. Encourage the body – Lift up

3. Comfort the body – Cheer up

4. Edify the body – Build up

## Prophetic Revelation

Prophecy is given only by revelation and not by personal effort or study. It cannot be overstated that no human effort, consultation, counsel or wisdom can give revelation. Revelation can only be revealed by the source. It is given by the Grace and Mercy of God.

> *"All things are delivered unto me of my father, an no man knoweth the son, but the father; neither knoweth any man the Father, save the son, and he to whomsoever the son will reveal him"*
> (St. Matthew 11:27).

> *"I am sought of them that asked not for me; I am found of them that sought me not: I said behold me, behold me, unto a nation that was not called by my name."* (Isiah 65:1).

God revealed himself to the Gentiles through the church, because his people either were not available, or not seeking to find him. This is more a statement of how much God wants himself to be known. The communication gap between God and man is not due to God, but man.

The ultimate revelation of God is in Christ Jesus. All other revelations either look back from that day, or look forward to his manifestation (as in the Old Testament).

There is no denying that much of the prophecies of the Old Testament was about the expected coming of Jesus Christ and the impact of his ministry. Here a few well known examples.

> *"For unto us a child is born, unto us a son is given: and the government shall be upon his shoulder: and his name shall be called Wonderful, counsellor, The Mighty God, The Everlasting Father, the Prince of Peace."* (Isaiah 9:6).

> *"The Sceptre shall not depart from Judah, nor a lawgiver from between his feet, until Shiloh come; and unto him shall the gathering of the people be."* (Genesis 49:10).

> *"And he made his grave with the wicked, and with the rich in his death; because he had done no violence, neither was any deceit in his mouth. Yet it pleased the Lord to bruise him; he hath put him to grief: when thou shalt make his soul an offering for sin, he shall see his seed, he shall prolong his days, and the pleasure of the Lord shall prosper in his hand."* (Isaiah 53:9-10).

Now that we are living in the Dispensation of the Holy Ghost, we know from experience that revelations of God will come in various ways. On one hand it may come at a time when we are not conscious of being in his presence. It may come while we are pursuing other things in our lives and in our own leisure time. On the other hand, it may come in the midst of adversity when we are being pressed on every side, or it may come during a time of prayer and supplication or while reading and meditating on his words. Why is that so? we may ask.

This is just so God can show he is sovereign. We do not set the parameters or framework within which God reveals himself.

Of course, when we place ourselves in a position of worship and adoration, we believe we are more likely to receive his revelations, but then again, we may not. Revelation is the sovereign work of God and comes when God determines it should.

Having said that, let us always try to '*set the mood*' for a revelation from God.

God speaks in various ways. Here are some that we have already encountered:

+ Directly, in an audible voice. This was the case with a young Samuel who heard the voice of God and inquired of Eli what he should do

+ Speaking through others. God may speak prophetically through his servant (this could be a prophet, our pastor, ministers in our assembly, or even through a perfect stranger)

+ Using our circumstances. As an example, God spoke to Elijah while he lay under a juniper tree, contemplating his own life, being dejected. I Kings 19:4-5.

+ Dreams (during sleep), Visions (while awake or in a trance). This was the case with Peter before he went to preach the Gospel to Cornelius' house and opened the door to the Gentiles. (Acts 10:10-16).

+ Everyday situations

+ During periods of emotional upheaval

† During prayer, fasting, worship

† Any number of different situations.

The more familiar we are with the voice of God, the more we will recognize it, regardless of what form it speaks. Like with all relationships, we learn more and more intimate details about the people in our lives the more time we spend with them. In a similar way we learn how to hear the voice of God and how to distinguish it from others.

Here are some guidelines to follow in the exercise of this gift:

The primary motive behind the exercise of the gift is Love.

> *"Follow after charity, and desire spiritual gifts, but rather that ye may prophesy"* (I Corinthians 14:1).

† There have been several instances where the exercise of this gift has been abused. So, be cautious.

† Paul warns that to safeguard against abuse, the gift should be restricted to two or three persons at any one time

> *"Let the prophets speak two or three, and let the other judge. If any thing be revealed to another that sitteth by, let the first hold his peace."* (I Corinthians 14:29-30).

† The word of prophecy may be delivered in different ways by different people. One person may bring a word of prophecy following speaking in tongues, while another may deliver the word without speaking in tongues. The fact that one individual delivers the word following speaking in tongues does not mean that is the only way it can be delivered. The fact that the word is delivered following a period of prolonged tongues, does

not make the word any more truthful, than if there were no tongues.

✝ The word of prophecy may be given, with or without emotion. It can be uttered loudly, quietly, in song, poetry or other means.

✝ A person who has received a word of prophecy is not bound to utter it instantaneously. There are times that the prophecy may be more appropriate for use at a latter occasion.

✝ The word of prophecy does not have a shelf life, unless God directs otherwise. There needs be no fear of forgetfulness. Sometimes the person who received the word of prophecy needs to discern what is the right timing for delivering that word. It is better to delay delivering a word of prophecy than to deliver that word in haste and inflict damage to the body of Christ.

✝ Remember, the spirit of the prophet is subject to the control of the prophet. (I Corinthians 14:32).

✝ There is no rule that when giving a word of prophecy, the word has to be introduced with: 'I am he Lord' or 'Thus saith the Lord' etc. It could simply be: 'I believe this is what the spirit of the Lord is saying to the church...'

✝ There is no rule that the language of the word of prophecy should be using biblical language such as: Whither, whosever, comest, goest, etc.

✝ There is no rule that the prophecy has to be given in a strange voice, and not the normal voice of the person giving the prophecy

† Equally, the fact that the person giving the word of prophecy is using their normal voice, does not invalidate the prophecy

† It is all about the spirit. Remember, we are all emotional beings, and we worship God with our emotions. We all express ourselves differently in general, so in a prophetic setting, we will all do so through different emotions.

CHAPTER FOURTEEN

# TEACHING

*"And he gave some, apostles; and some, prophets; and some, evangelists; and some, pastors and teachers."* (Ephesians 4:11).

### Gift Definition

**The Gift of Teaching enables one to instruct others in a systematic way, as to communicate information leading to true understanding of scripture and growth.**

---

Teaching is one of the gifts that God gives to the body of Christ that elevates to the level of a Ministry. The others are the Apostle, Prophet, Evangelist and Pastor. These gifts, working together are essential for the perfecting of the saints, for the work of the Ministry for the edifying of the body of Christ.

I once heard a preacher describe the working of the fivefold ministries as: The Apostles Govern, the Prophets Guard, the Evangelists Gathers, the Pastor Guides and the Teacher Grounds the church.

If we should cast our minds back to when we were children, growing up, some of the people who have had the greatest impact and influence on our lives are teachers.

I still remember Mrs. Homer, my grade 3 teacher, who drilled me into memorizing nursery rhymes, poems, songs and what we called *"times table"* i.e. 2 times $1 = 2$, 2 times $2 = 4$, all the way up to 12 times $12 = 144$.

Better yet, it was Ms. Carrington, my grade 5 teacher who taught me the concept of an atom, and explained the nucleus, and how the electrons revolved around the nucleus.

By far, the most influential person in my school life is my fourth Form Mathematics teacher – Keith Irons. For the most part his teaching methods were so motivating to me that I decided then and there that I wanted to be an engineer. I wanted to be immersed in mathematics for the rest of my life.

I still use his name sometimes for passwords to some of my electronic files (this is not a license for the reader to hack into my online account).

Setting all jokes aside, teachers who have crossed paths with us through our lives are integral to our ultimate career choices and life goals. I have had numerous conversations with students who are struggling with certain subjects. Inevitably, when I trace the origin of their learning difficult, it goes back to an encounter they had with a teacher who was either not their favourite, or they felt that teacher did a poor job of teaching the basics of that subject. Many such students never recover and perform poorly in that subject throughout their life.

There is a lot to be said about those who bury themselves into learning with the sole intention or for the sole purpose of disseminating what they have studied to help others. Not only are teachers desirous that students learn what is being taught, teachers aim for the student to learn so well that the student is able to teach it. By so doing the learning cycle continues, and knowledge is propagated and keeps feeding itself.

The biblical word for teacher is derived from the Greek - didaskalos. This word is translated as Master, mainly in the gospels (except in Luke 2:46), but always as teacher in the Epistles. With the occurrence of this word in Romans, Corinthians and Ephesians, we will only consider the word in the context of Teacher in our study.

For the purpose of our study, we will use the definition of the teacher as:

> *One who teaches concerning the things of God, and the Duties of Man.*

It is a fact that in order to gain proficiency in any subject area, one has to dedicate themselves to a systematic program of study, usually proceeding from basic to more complex matter. Every school, college, university, institution of higher learning is a testament of this fact. It is no different for those who are teachers of biblical truths. There must first be knowledge of God, which comes by receiving the Spirit of God. After that, there must be a systematic program of study of the words of God, as outlined in the bible.

Many of the great teachers of our day commenced the journey in a bible teaching bible-believing bible-centered Sunday School. During those formative years, foundational principles are entrenched in young lives. I still remember learning by recitation of scriptures. Many scriptures we learned in Sunday School, still remains in our consciousness.

It was during those formative years that many of us learned about the Oneness of God, as echoed in the old testament:

> *"Hear Oh Israel, the Lord our God is one Lord."*
> (Deuteronomy 6:4).

Teachers grow out of childhood into adulthood, and learn more about God by association, experience, fasting and prayer, study and daily attendance to the church where the word is constantly preached. The qualities that distinguishes the teacher from their peers, is the un-quenched desire and thirst for the word of God. Often the teacher is al-ways questioning what others are prepared to accept at face value. The teacher is inquisitive and desires more. The teacher often goes the extra step to seek out knowledge and will often end up in a Bible College.

Solomon's writing is a fitting description of the teacher:

> *"My son if thou will receive my words, and hide my*
> *commandments with thee: so that thou incline thine ear unto*
> *wisdom, and apply thine heart to understanding: yea, if thou*
> *criest after knowledge, and liftest up thy voice for understanding:*
> *if thou seekest her as silver, and searchest for her as for hid*
> *treasures: then shall thou understand the fear of the Lord, and*
> *find the knowledge of God."* (Proverbs 2:1-5).

It is important to note that the mere pursuit of the word of God is not an indication of the presence of the teaching gift in an individual. As ad-mittedly many have spent countless time and effort reading and study-ing scriptures, but do not operate in this gift. Those individuals will benefit from the full knowledge of the word of God, even though they are not teachers.

The individual who operates in the gift has the Holy Spirit as an illu-minator of those things which they have studied. In addition, the spirit gives the anointing to enable the teacher to impart the words and to instruct the learner in special God enhanced ways.

The writer could easily provide a list of things to the reader, in an at-tempt to guide those gifted in the Teaching Ministry, to enable them to make full proof of their ministry. But why bother. We have the example to follow. One who has modelled the way to do this.

After all, he is the greatest teacher ever to walk the earth. Jesus Christ. Master, Rabbi. The best advice I can give is that teachers or those working in the teaching ministry or in the office of the teacher, adopt the pattern given by Jesus Christ.

So, how did Jesus Christ go about teaching? For the answers to this question, I have summarized extracts from a paper by Michel G. England, submitted in partial fulfillment for Christology, as follows:

- Jesus began where people were

   The idea here is that students learns new truths through old ones, or goes from the known to the unknown. The truth to be taught must be learned through truths already known.

- Jesus Christ worked on the conscience.

   He made his appeal to the conscience: that is, one's sense of obligation or sensitivity to right or wrong. He worked on the conscience more that the intellect. He made truths compelling. People went away from his teaching feeling something should be done about it.

- Jesus Christ drew out the best out of people

   Whether it was a self-righteous Pharisee, a deceitful Tax-collector or a fallen woman (caught in adultery), he appealed to the finer nature and elicited the good. He did so by stressing their future possibilities, showing an interest in them and inspiring them to achieve the good. He believed that the way to get faith out of men is to show that you have faith in them.

Here are some examples of the forms and techniques Christ used:

# OVERSTATEMENT (HYPERBOLE)

In this technique, Jesus overstated that truth in a way that the resulting exaggeration brought home the point. This method shocked the hearers and demanded a response. Some examples are:

> *"If any man come to me and hate not his father, and mother, and wife, and children, and brethren, and sisters, yea, and his own life also, he cannot be my disciples."* (Luke 14:26).

> *"And if thy right eye offends thee, pluck it out, and cast it from thee; For it is profitable for thee that one of thy members should perish, and not thy whole body should be cast into hell. And if thy right hand offends thee, cut it off, and cast it from thee: for it is profitable for thee that one of thy members should perish, and not that thy whole body should be cast into hell."*
> (Matthew 5: 29-30).

# SIMILE

A simile is a comparison between two things that are essentially unlike each other and are connected to each other by "like" or "as" or "than." Here is an example:

> *"Behold I send you forth as sheep in the midst of wolves: be ye therefore wise as serpents, and harmless as doves."*
> (Matthew 10:16).

## SPOKE WITH AUTHORITY

Here are some examples of this:

> *"But I say unto you, that whosoever is angry with his brother without a cause shall be in danger of the judgment: and whosoever shall say to this brother Raca, shall be in danger of the counsel: but whosoever shall say, thou fool, shall be in danger of hell fire."* (Matthew 5:22).

> *"But I say unto you, that whosoever looketh on a woman to lust after her hath committed adultery with her already in his heart."* (Matthew 5:28).

> *"But I say unto you, love your enemies, bless them that curse you, do good to them that hate you, and pray for them which despitefully use you, and persecute you."* (Matthew 5:44).

## JESUS TOLD STORIES

Actually, he spoke parables which are literal stories that have a moral or spiritual meaning and application. Jesus used the illustration of the "Prodigal Son" in Luke 15: 11-32, to illustrate the greater point of the joy in the presence of the angels of God over one sinner that repents.

## JESUS CRAFTED MEMORABLE SAYINGS

Some examples are:

*"Give and it will come back to you, good measure, pressed down and shaken together and running over."* (St. Luke 6:38).

*"Judge not that ye be not judged.* (Matthew 7:1).

## JESUS ASKED QUESTIONS

The questions Jesus asked were pointed. They were so impactful and thought- provoking. It always required soul-searching and demanded an answer. Examples are:

*"For what is a man profited, if he shall gain the whole world, and loose his own soul? Or what shall a man give in exchange for his own soul?"* (Matthew 16:26)

## JESUS USED VISUAL ILLUSTRATIONS

- † He washed his disciples' feet

- † He used a little child to illustrate the attitudes that should be displayed in the Kingdom of Heaven

- † Jesus used his observation of the contributions to the treasury to illustrate that the widow's two mites was worth more than that of all the others, for it was her whole livelihood

## JESUS USED REPETITIONS

On several occasions he repeated the imminent event of his death, burial and resurrection. See Mark 8:31, 9:31 and 10:33-34.

## JESUS CREATED MEMORABLE EXPERIENCES

Jesus created experiences so his disciples had live experiences of what Jesus instilled in them. On at least two occasions, Jesus authorized his disciples to go with the gospel, heal the sick, cleanse lepers, raise the dead, and then received a report from them on their return.

## JESUS PRACTISED WHAT HE PREACHED

Not only did Jesus encouraged and commanded his disciples to pray, but he taught them how to pray and set the example:

> *"And he withdrew himself into the wilderness, and prayed."*
> (Luke 5:16).

Jesus commanded and encouraged his disciples to love and display humility.

> *"So after he had washed their feet, and had taken his garments, and was set down again, he said unto them, know ye what I have done to you? Ye call me master and lord: and ye say well; for so I am. If I then, your lord and master, have washed your feet; ye also ought to wash one another's feet. For I have given you an example, that ye should do as I have done."* (John 13:12-15).

CHAPTER FIFTEEN

# WORD OF KNOWLEDGE

*"And there are diversities of operations, but it is the same God which worketh all in all. But the manifestation of the Spirit is given to ever man to profit withal. For to one is given by the spirit the word of wisdom, to another the word of knowledge by the same spirit. To another faith by the same Spirit, to another the gifts of healing by the same Spirit. To another the working of miracles; to another prophecy; to another discerning of spirits; to another diverse kinds of tongues; to another the interpretation of tongues":* (I Corinthians 12: 6-10).

### Gift Definition

**Word of Knowledge is the revelation of facts about a person or situation, which is not learned through the efforts of the natural mind, but is a fragment of knowledge given by God. During this revelation, truth is disclosed so as to edify the body of Christ.**

---

The general acquisition of knowledge is to seek to learn (acquire) as much about a subject (in this case the bible) as possible, through the gathering of information and analyzing data.

Knowledge as defined in the Greek – ginosko, to learn, to know.

This knowledge can be one of the following:

&dagger;   To understand, perceive, have knowledge of

&dagger;   Jewish idiom for sexual intercourse between a man and a woman

&dagger;   To become acquainted with

In contrast however, The Word of Knowledge is different from resident knowledge or acquired knowledge (head knowledge). It is not knowledge of explanation. Instead, it is illuminated knowledge, only available at a *chiros* time (time of opportunity). It is:

&dagger;   Knowledge to match an immediate opportunity

&dagger;   Knowledge given to meet an immediate need and only applicable to that need

&dagger;   It is instantaneous knowledge

&dagger;   It is spiritual insight

&dagger;   It is only available by the spirit

Word of Knowledge is not previously unrevealed truth concerning the person of Jesus, the Godhead, the way of Salvation or revelation contrary to the holy scriptures. In other words, there can be no new revelations that contradicts existing revelations about God. This should not be a surprise if we note the scriptures as follows:

*"For other foundations can no man lay than that is laid."*
(I Corinthians 3:11).

*"But though we, or an angel from heaven, preach any other
gospel unto you than that ye have received, let him be accursed."*
(Galatians 1:8).

*"And are built upon the foundation of he apostles and prophets,
Jesus Christ himself being the chief corner stone;"*
(Ephesians 2:20).

Based on these scriptures, the believer must rule out fringe groups or sects that have reportedly received special revelations or acquired secret knowledge of a new approach to serve God. It also rules out knowledge of new revelations concerning the person of Jesus Christ and the truth of the godhead.

Now, let us distinguish that there exist non-natural knowledge as follows:

**Psychics**, who have presented knowledge relating to or denoting faculties or phenomenon that are inexplicable by natural laws.

**The Occult,** that has engaged in *'supernatural'* mystical or magical practices or phenomenon. This may include magic, black-magic, witchcraft, sorcery, necromance, wizardry.

**The Metaphysical** has engaged in acts that transcend laws of nature, including levitation, astral projection, out-of-body experience.

These are all disqualified as Words of knowledge as they are clearly not motivated by, or illuminated by the Spirit of God, but by other sources. Sources that God warned his people in Israel to avoid. See the brief answer to the question 6 at the end of this book.

The Gift of the Word of Knowledge comes from and through the Holy Spirit to our spirit and reveals something of the mind of God to profit and benefit one another. It may concern the past, present or the future.

Perhaps the best way to introduce Word of Knowledge is to provide examples of this gift in use in scriptures:

1.  The revelation to Jesus of the background of the Woman at the well and his statement to her.

    *"For thou hast had five husbands; and he whom thou now hast is not thy husband: in that saidst thou truly."* (St. John 4:18).

2.  The revelation to Peter of deception and lying of Ananias and Sapphira and his response to them.

    *"But Peter said, Ananias, why hath Satan filled thine heart to lie to the Holy Ghost, and to keep back part of the price of the land?" Then Peter said unto her, how is it that ye have agreed together to tempt the Spirit of the Lord? Behold, the feet of them which have buried thy husband are at the door, and shall carry thee out."* (Acts 5:3,9).

3.  An indication of a suitable meeting place for hosting the last supper (Passover).

    *"And he sendeth forth two of his disciples and saith unto them, go ye into the city, and there shall meet you a man bearing a pitcher of water: follow him. And wheresoever he shall go in, say ye to the good-man of the house, the master saith, where is the guest-chamber, where I shall eat the Passover with my disciples? And he will shew you a large upper room furnished and prepared: there make ready for us."* (St. Mark 14:13-15).

4. A revelation that a 4-drachma coin is to be found in the mouth of a fish, so Peter could then catch the fish, remove the coin and pay required taxes.

   *"Notwithstanding, lest we should offend them, go thou to the sea, and cast an hook, and take up the fish that first cometh up; and when thou hast opened his mouth, thou shalt find a piece of money: that take, and give unto them for me and thee."*
   (St. Matthew 17:27).

5. A revelation of the kind of demon troubling an epileptic boy. The father said it was dumb, but Jesus said it was deaf and dumb.

   *" And one of the multitude answered and said, Master, I have brought unto thee my son, which hath a dumb spirit; When Jesus saw that the people came running together, he rebuked the foul spirit, saying unto him, thou dumb and deaf spirit, I charge thee, come out of him, and enter no more into him."*
   (St. Mark 9:17,25).

## Different ways how the Gift is Received

1. The gift may be given by God, without the individual asking for that gift.

   *"But all these worketh that one and the selfsame Spirit, dividing to every man severally as he will."* (I Corinthians 12:11)

2. It may be requested from God.

   *"And I say unto you, ask, and it shall be given you: seek, and ye shall find; knock, and it shall be opened unto you."*
   (St. Luke 11:9)

3. In ministering to others, it may be right to ask for this gift

4. It may be imparted through another who has the gift.

   *"For I long to see you, that I may impart unto you some spiritual gift, to the end ye may be established;"* (Romans 1:11).

5. Paul encouraged Timothy to fan the flame of the gift of God.

   *"Wherefore I put thee in remembrance that thou stir up the gift of God, which is in thee by the putting on of my hands."*
   (II Timothy 1:6).

This impartation does not only apply to the Word of Knowledge, but to all spiritual gifts.

CHAPTER SIXTEEN
# WORD OF WISDOM

*"And there are diversities of operations, but it is the same God which worketh all in all. But the manifestations of the Spirit is given to ever man to profit withal. For to one is given by the spirit the word of wisdom, to another the word of knowledge by the same spirit. To another faith by the same Spirit, to another the gifts of healing by the same Spirit. To another the working of miracles; to another prophecy; to another discerning of spirits; to another diverse kinds of tongues; to another the interpretation of tongues;"* (I Corinthians 12: 6-10).

## Gift Definition

**This Gift refers to the special ability given by the spirit how to apply knowledge in such a way to make spiritual truths to a particular situation or need arising in the body of Christ.**

---

Wisdom can generally be referred to as application of knowledge. So, using that definition, there will always be an association between wisdom and knowledge. One definition from scripture is that wisdom is the comprehension of learning.

Wisdom by the Spirit of God is one of three departments of knowledge among Hebrews, the others being the law and prophecy. The law presents the commandments and claims of God to man; prophecy passes judgment on conduct in the light of God's revealed will with men; wisdom seeks by observation, experience, and reflection to know things in their essence and reality as they stand related to man and God.

Four kinds of wisdom can be distinguished:

1.  Human Wisdom which is naturally applied to knowledge. Such wisdom, rightly used can contribute to human progress. However, it also panders to man's pride. For that reason, the scripture states:

    *"I will destroy the wisdom of the wise; bring to nothing  the understanding (intelligence) of the prudent."*
    (I Corinthians 1:19).

2.  The fallen world's supernatural wisdom. This was one basis of the first temptation when the woman saw that the forbidden fruit was '*desirable for gaining wisdom*' and '*took and ate it*' (Genesis 3:6). Such wisdom is strictly forbidden by God.

At the tower of Babel:

> *"And they said, go to, let us build us a city and a tower, whose top may reach unto heaven; and let us make us a name, lest we be scattered abroad upon the face of the whole earth. And the Lord came down to see the city and the tower, which the children of men builded. And the Lord said, behold, the people is one, and they have all one language; and this they begin to do: and now nothing will be restrained from them, which they have imagined to do. Go to, let us go down, and there confound their language, that they may not understand one another's speech."*(Genesis 11:4-11).

3.  Spiritual Wisdom such is exemplified in the book of proverbs, and we are told to seek to acquire of God. Ultimately, Christ is the wisdom of God I Corinthians 1:24. Scriptures state:

    *"If any of you lack wisdom, let him ask of God, that giveth to all men liberally, and upbraideth not; and it shall be given him."* (*James 1:5*). *Paul prayed: "For this cause we also, since the day we heard it, do not cease to pray for you, and to desire that ye might be filled with the knowledge of his will in all wisdom and spiritual understanding."* (Colossians 1:9).

4.  Then there is the Word of Wisdom. This is the miraculous giving of wisdom to meet a given situation, answer a particular question or utilize a particular bit of knowledge, natural or supernatural.

Perhaps one of the most outstanding examples that identify the word of wisdom is the case Solomon resolved with two women and their babies. Both women came to Solomon with their babies, one dead, one alive. Each mother claimed the living to be their own. Through a 'Word of Wisdom' Solomon was able to publicly resolve the problems, by suggesting the living child be cut in two. Whilst one mother agreed, the other pleaded that the first mother keep the baby.

Solomon ordered the baby to be given to the latter.

> *"And the king said, Divide the living child in two, and give half to the one, and half to the other"* (I Kings 3:25).

This was in fact a word of wisdom.

Jesus himself manifested Words of Wisdom on several occasions. Here are some examples:

1.  His response to the question of his authority:

    *"And when he was come into the temple, the chief priests and the elders of the people came unto him as he was teaching, and said, by what authority doest thou these things? And who gave thee this authority? And Jesus answered and said unto them, I also will ask you one thing, which if ye tell me, I in like wise will tell you by what authority I do these things. The baptism of John, whence was it? From heaven, or of men? And they reasoned with themselves, saying, if we shall say, from heaven, he will say unto us, why did you not then believe him? But if we shall say, of men; we fear the people; for all hold John as a prophet. And they answered Jesus, and said, we cannot tell. And he said unto them, neither tell I you by what authority I do these things."* (St. Matthew 21:23-27).

2.  The way he answered the question of paying taxes:

    *"Then went the Pharisees, and took counsel how they might entangle him in his talk. And they sent out unto him their disciples with Herodians, saying, master, we know thou art true, and teachest the way of God in truth, neither carest thou for any man: for thou regardest not the person of men. Tell us therefore, what thinkest thou? Is it lawful to give tribute unto Caesar, or not? But Jesus perceived their wickedness, and said, why tempt ye me, ye hypocrites? Show me the tribute money, and they brought unto him a penny. And he saith unto them, whose is this image and superscription?*

*They say unto him, Caesar's. Then saith he unto them, render therefore unto Caesar the things which are Caesar's; and unto God the things that are God's."* (St. Matthew 22:15-21).

CHAPTER SEVENTEEN

# TONGUES

*"And there are diversities of operations, but it is the same God
which worketh all in all. But the manifestations of the Spirit
is given to ever man to profit withal. For to one is given by the
spirit the word of wisdom, to another the word of knowledge by
the same spirit. To another faith by the same Spirit, to another
the gifts of healing by the same Spirit. To another the working of
miracles; to another prophecy; to another discerning of spirits; to
another diverse kinds of tongues; to another the interpretation of
tongues;"* (I Corinthians 12: 6-10).

*"If any man speaks in an unknown tongue, let it be by two, or at
the most by three, and that by course; and let one interpret. But if
there be no interpreter, let him keep silence in the church; and let
him speak to himself, and to God."* (I Corinthians 14: 27-28).

### Gift Definition

**To speak in a language not previously learned so that
unbelievers can hear God's message in their own language
or so the body of Christ may be edified.**

The Greek word translated tongues in Acts 2:11 has the translation of - *"Language"*.

Using that definition, we could come to the conclusion that the Gift of Tongues has to do with the ability to communicate the Gospel in other languages.

The Gift of Tongues is one of the most unique and intriguing of the spiritual gifts. It duplicates an event that occurred in the upper room on the Day of Pentecost.

> *"And they were all filled with the Holy Ghost, and began to speak with other tongues, as the Spirit gave them utterance."* (Acts 2:4).

For the first time, men who were known to be Galileans spoke in the language of seventeen other nations. The language they spoke in was not known to those speaking the language, but was known to the hearers. The hearers knew these Galileans had no opportunity to learn the many different languages which they heard them speaking. This feat could only be accomplished by the Spirit of God.

God choose to establish that the human instrument that would be the symbol to manifest the Holy Ghost is the tongue. Isaiah prophesied of this day and this experience. He said:

> *"For with stammering lips and another tongue will he speak to this people. To whom he said, this is the rest wherewith ye may cause the weary to rest; and this is the refreshing: yet they would not hear."* (Isaiah 28:11, 12).

The importance of tongues as the initial evidence of the Holy Ghost is carefully validated in scripture. In three of the five accounts in Acts of people being filled with the Holy Ghost, it was specifically stated that they spoke in other tongues (Acts 2:4; 10:44-46; 19:1-7).

Let us establish the facts about speaking in tongues

- † Speaking in tongues is the initial evidence of the infilling of the Holy Spirit

- † Everyone who received the Holy Spirit speaks in tongues

- † The fact that one speaks in tongues having received the Holy Spirit is not one and the same as that individual having the Gift of Tongues

- † Not everyone who speaks in tongues has the Gift of Tongues

- † Everyone who has the Gift of Tongues, does speak in tongues outside of the operation of the gift

- † The Gift of Tongues was not in operation in the Old Testament

There are three (3) distinctions in the tongues that scriptures have identified:

1. This tongue is unknown to the speaker but known to the hearers. This is the case in Acts 2:4, and needs no interpretation

2. Tongues that is unknown to both speaker and hearers and needs interpretation so that the hearers can be edified. This kind of tongues is addressed by Paul in I Corinthians 14: 27.

3. Tongues that are spoken to God and not for the benefit of the hearers. This is often the case in public worship services, where there is free, unrestrained worship. This kind of tongue is communication between and individual and God. It is unknown to the speaker, unknown to the hearer, but known to God.

There is no need for interpretation. Paul addressed this kind of tongues in I Corinthians 14:2.

The fact that scriptures have identified three distinctions in tongues raises the valid question, how do you know when an individual speaks in tongues, which of the three applies?

This goes to the heart of why those operating in the Gift of Tongues needs to be mature in the exercise of their gift, and why the Gift of Discernment needs to be at work simultaneously.

This is also the reason why this gift is one of the most abused gifts in the body of Christ and why this gift is tabooed in some churches. Some church leaders have made the decision to shut down the operation of this gift, because it is being operated without control, being mis-used and there is lack of clarity. The end result is the body of Christ is not being edified and unsaved are confused and speak ill of the operation of the Spirit.

For this reason, Paul in I Corinthians 14, has put some guidelines in place to help to manage the operation and application of this gift in the church. Is it fair to rob the body of Christ of a Gift that God placed in the Church for edification, simply because it is being abused or misused? No. Instead of eliminating this gift, Paul instructs that its use be regulated. Here are some guidelines:

Where the tongue is not understood by the speaker, but understood by an unbelieving bystander, it is meant to be a 'sign' of the Kingdom of God:

> *"Wherefore tongues are for a sign, not to them that believe, but to them that believe not: but prophesying serveth not for them that believe not, bot for them which believe."* (I Corinthians 14:22)

*"And they were all amazed, and were in doubt, saying one to another, What meaneth this?"* (Acts 2:12).

Tongues used in public, such as in services, enables the church to function as a body. Different members are involved. One speaks, another interprets.

*"If any man speak in an unknown tongue, let it be by tow, or at the most by three, and that by course; and let one interpret.* (I Corinthians 14:27).

In order to avoid confusion and expose the church to uncertainty about what God is saying, Paul encourages that whenever there are tongues, it be followed by interpretation. He further warns that if there is no independent person to interpret the tongues, the burden rests on the one who spoke in the unknown tongue to interpret it.

*"But if there be no interpreter, let him keep silence in the church; and let him speak to himself, and to God. Let the prophets speak two or three, and let the other judge."* (I Corinthians 14:28-29).

It is not uncommon for others to also have been given the burden of the interpretation, especially if they have asked God for it. One or two other persons may confirm the message in tongues and then one person gives the interpretation. If there is no interpretation, Paul admonishes that public proclaiming of unknown tongues be avoided, except in circumstances when tongues are being expressed directly to God.

There are a number of things at play here. It is clear that various gifts have to be at work in order for the Gift of Tongues to be effectively utilized to the edification of the church. Paul mentions the prophet as the one speaking in tongues. There is also the need for the gift of Interpretation of Tongues to be in operation.

It is clear therefore, that if the congregation is immature and there is no evidence of the other gifts of the spirit in manifestation, the operation of the Gift of Tongues will result in confusion and not edify the body of Christ.

In such cases, the church should be properly taught on the operation of this gift and there should be some confidence that there is a minimum level of maturity present, before this gift is unleashed in the body. Failure to do so can cause irreparable damage, from which it may be difficult to recover.

There is a danger in releasing this gift in a congregation that is ill-equipped. Many churches have had to learn this lesson the hard way.

On the other side of this argument, when the gifts are working harmoniously in the body, there is great benefit to be derived. One person speaks in an unknown tongue, another person confirms the message brought by the first in an unknown tongue, then a third person interprets that message. At the same time that the tongues and interpretation is going on (in courses, in order), others with the gift of discernment, have received confirmation of what the interpretation is, but hold their peace. Receiving the confirmation is sufficient, and needs no outward utterance.

When that happens, the body is edified, the unbelievers in the audience witness a move of God, and is sometimes brought to conviction.

Regardless of whether one has the maturity to operate in this gift in public setting, tongues have been utilized extensively by individuals as a means of private communication with God.

> "For he that speaketh in an unknown tongue speaketh not unto men, but unto God: for no man undestandeth him; howbeit in the spirit he speaketh mysteries." (I Corinthians 14:2).

In this way, tongues express a verbal intimacy with God, in so doing provides a new dimension in a person's prayer life. It is a prayer language which no man can understand, but only God.

Consequently, such prayer cannot be hindered by opposing spiritual forces. This can be contrasted with Daniel's experience in Daniel 10.

Tongues is also used a means of prayer intercession where through tongues, the Spirit intercedes for us in a manner that we are unable to:

> *"Likewise the Spirit also helpeth or infirmities: for we know not what we should pray for as we ought: but the Spirit itself maketh intercession for us with groanings which cannot be uttered."*
> (Romans 8:26).

Finally, tongues are one of our greatest weapon when we engage in Spiritual Warfare. During times of personal conflict, or when ministering to others in the area of deliverance, or perhaps when casting out demons. The Gift of Tongues is deployed very effectively in speaking to spiritual conditions that may not be known, or apparent to the untrained eye.

Paul encourages us as follows:

> *"Praying always with all prayer and supplication in the Spirit, and watching thereunto with all perseverance and supplication for all saints:"* (Ephesians 6:18).

CHAPTER EIGHTEEN

# INTERPRETATION OF TONGUES

*"And there are diversities of operations, but it is the same God which worketh all in all. But the manifestations of the Spirit is given to ever man to profit withal. For to one is given by the spirit the word of wisdom, to another the word of knowledge by the same spirit. To another faith by the same Spirit, to another the gifts of healing by the same Spirit. To another the working of miracles; to another prophecy; to another discerning of spirits; to another diverse kinds of tongues; to another the interpretation of tongues;"* (I Corinthians 12: 6-10).

*"If any man speak in an unknown tongue, let it be by two, or at the most by three, and that by course; and let one interpret. But if there be no interpreter, let him keep silence in the church; and let him speak to himself, and to God."* (I Corinthians 14: 27-28).

### Gift Definition

**The supernatural revelation through the Holy Spirit which enables the believer to interpret the message of someone who has spoken in Tongues.**

The Gift of Interpretation of Tongues is closely related the Gift of Tongues. In fact, in most circumstances, this gift is a companion to the gift of tongues.

Paul instructs that those operating in the gift of tongues should seek the interpretation of the tongues in which they prophecy.

The gift of interpretation of tongues is probably one of the most subjective of all the spiritual gifts. To a large extent, it depends largely on the person interpreting the tongues. Every individual has different ways of expressing themselves, so that the same tongues are likely to be interpreted in two different ways by two people, even if both operate in the Gift.

Let us examine the uniqueness of this gift:

† Interpretation is not an operation of the mind of the interpreter, but of the mind of God

† Interpretation is just as much a supernatural manifestation as the original utterance in tongues

† The congregation will remain un-edified by a tongue if there is no interpretation, or if the interpretation is an error

† Paul forbids the continued use of tongues without an interpretation

† Interpretation is not translation, nor transliteration

† Interpretation is not an exercise in language

† Interpretation does not conform to rules of syntax, form, word structure or origin

✝ The interpretation of tongues may be shorter or longer than the original tongues. The fact that it does not match in the length of time does not invalidate the interpretation

✝ The tongue can be given in language of scripture, while the interpretation can be given in today's language

✝ The interpretation of tongues may just convey the essence of the message

✝ The interpreter may only receive the burden of the tongue

As discussed in the previous chapter, Paul addressed both those prophesying in tongues and the need for interpretation of tongues in I Corinthians 14.

In order to ensure harmony in the working of all gifts, there may be times when tongues are spoken and there is no interpretation. Paul instructs that we should pray for the interpretation in such instances.

Here are some points to consider:

1. Greater faith is needed for interpretation than for speaking in tongues. Whereas the tongue is usually unintelligible, the interpretation is given publicly for the edification of the whole congregation and must be understood and tested by all.

2. It is often beneficial if the person conducting the service during the utterance of tongues is experienced and knowledgeable on the operation of the gifts in the church.

3. The person who speaks in tongues should also pray for the interpretation, but his is not limited to the person who spoke the

tongues. All those others who speak in tongues should also be praying for the interpretation.

4. At times one person may be given the first part of the interpretation and another given the words to continue or terminate. But care must be taken here because it may become tempting for people to 'outdo' each other in interpretation.

5. If the gifts are working harmoniously, everything will be done in order and those interpreting the tongues will not contradict each other, or will not bring a contrary interpretation. For this reason, Paul admonishes:

*"Let all things be done decently and in order."*
(I Corinthians 14:40).

One final note on interpretation of tongues. There may be occasions when there may be a need to contradict an interpretation. When and if that happens, this will come through the Gift of Discernment.

It is quite acceptable to bring the church to order and explain what the mind of the spirit has discerned, and bring to an end an interpretation that is in error. Once again, it cannot be overstated, that if there is uncertainty about what is the interpretation, or it is unclear what is the mind of the Spirit, hold your peace. If it of God, it will stand. God will find a way to reveal it. After all it is his church.

CHAPTER NINETEEN

# WRAP-UP

A study of Spiritual Gifts cannot be considered complete without including a discussion of Love. Interestingly, Love is not stated as one of the Spiritual Gifts that God placed in the Church. What then should we say about love and its role in the effective manifestation and operation of our spiritual gifts?

God is uniquely who he is by virtue of his characteristics and qualities.

These include:

God is Omniscient

God is Omnipotent

God is Omnipresent

God is Holy

God is Immutable

God is Eternal

God is Righteous

God is Love

Love can be characterised as an attribute, but extends to the expression of God's nature.

> *"God is love; and he that dwelleth in love dwelleth in God, and God in him."* (I John 4:16).

> *"For God so loved the world, that he gave his only begotten son, that whosoever believeth in him should not perish, but have everlasting life."* (St. John 3:16).

To say that God is Love is to be understood in the same sense as "God is light" (I John 1:5) and "God is a Spirit" (St. John 4:24). These statements do not just speak of things about God or about his character but speak to the very essence of his being.

Interestingly Paul's writing to the Corinthians addresses the matter of spiritual gifts in Chapter 12. In chapter 14, he goes on to address the operation of the gifts, placing emphasis on prophesying, tongues and interpretation of tongues. Carefully sandwiched between these two chapters, Paul addresses the whole matter of Love. In fact, he admonishes the church to follow after love in the pursuit and operation of spiritual gifts. Is this coincidental? Of course not.

Paul seems to have devoted a great deal of time to address the matter of tongues in this epistle (12:10, 28,30; 13:1; 14:2, 4-25). Some have come to the conclusion that some Corinthian Christians count speaking in tongues as the most significant of the gifts, and became proud about their ability to speak and interpret tongues.

While Paul recognize the importance of the spiritual gifts and the purpose they serve in the body of Christ and their role in edifying the body of Christ, he instructs that there is something more important than these gifts. He proceeds to make the argument that without love the other gifts do not have much value. In essence, if the spiritual gifts are to serve their God given purpose to the body, they must be mixed in with Love.

He alludes to the temporary nature of the spiritual gifts and the contrasting permanence of Love as shown in the following scripture:

> *"Charity never faileth: but whether there be prophecies, they shall fail; whether there is tongues, they shall cease; whether there be knowledge, it shall vanish away."* (I Corinthians 13:8).

While Faith, Hope and Love will endure but Love is superior to all.

On close examination I Corinthians 13 is just another way to describe the Fruit of the Spirit.

CHAPTER TWENTY
# QUESTION & ANSWERS

## Question 1

What if I pursue what I feel is my gift, but it turns out not to be my gift, how much damage can that do to the individual?

## Answer

If you pursue doing something that turns out not to be your gift, that does not have to end badly. It can be compared to experience. All experience is good. At least the individual will have learned a new skill, which is always going to be beneficial. Having said that, notice that Paul in 1 Corinthians 14:1 encourages us to covet the best gift. It means therefore, we can adopt gifts that are not really 'ours' and can make full proof of our ministry in that adopted gifts. I have known of many Pastors who have found themselves pastoring out of a need. They are the first to admit they are not 'pastor' but adapted them self to that ministry to fill a need that was created.

Of course, I would have to question how you came to the conclusion that is not your gift. God does work in mysterious ways, and sometimes, we are incorrect in our conclusion as to what is 'our' gift.

# Question 2

Do you have any suggestions on ways to help those who are searching for answers regarding developing and manifesting in their spiritual gift?

# Answer

A great way is to place individuals in a team, working on a project together. Such projects may be; developing a department organizational chart, planning a department retreat, coordinate a special service, outdoor evangelism activity and program for those leaning towards Administrative type gifts. For other gifts, they can get involved in prayer or fasting service, working at the altar, visiting the sick, deliverance ministry, laying on of hands, etc. When placed in a role where some mentorship is provided, persons who are exploring their gift can have the benefit of learning from and asking question of people who have demonstrated experience in that particular area and are active. One of the best way to learn is by doing.

Jesus did not only perform miracles in the presence of his disciples, but he sent them to do the same things he did. He had them report to him on their experience.

Regarding mentorship, we should approach this not as a static, one-time interaction with those seeking to explore their gift. In addition, mentorship needs not be one-way, where the mentor pursues the mentee. Those seeking mentorship should also seek out mentors and ask for help and guidance in moving through stages of their development in a gifting. The mentor/mentee relationship should continue until the mentee has moved through the various stages of development, into maturity.

# Question 3

What is your opinion on those who are called apostles today?

# Answer

In order accurately answer this question we must resolve two things:

1.  The number of Apostles and,

2.  The duties of the Apostles

It is clear from the fact that Christ called twelve apostles that this is consistent with God's Governmental principles, twelve being God's governmental number. Scriptures bears this out that the church is built on this principle:

> *"And the wall of the city had twelve foundations, and in them the names of the twelve apostles of the lamb."* (Revelations 21:14)

So there is consistency in scripture that the number twelve for the apostles was designated by God. We know however, that there were other men, not in the original twelve that were Apostles. Paul as an example, was not. Later, in the Churches that formed during the first century we learn of others such as Titus, Barnabas, Silas and Timothy.

When Judas committed suicide after betraying Christ, another apostle was selected to replace him. When looking for qualified men, the apostles narrowed the choices to two men.

However, they knew they could only select one: It appeared that it was important that the number of apostles remain at twelve.

Even though Paul was not one of the original twelve, we see how he obtained his apostleship. Paul himself stated he was an apostle. He recounts his experience of being an eyewitness of Jesus' resurrection (I Corinthians 9:1; 15:3-10). He was able to give proof of his apostleship by the signs God gave to accompany him

> *"Truly the signs of an apostle were wrought among you in all patience, in signs, and wonders, and mighty deeds"* (II Corinthians 12:12).

In relation to the Apostles' duties, beyond serving as eyewitnesses of Christ's resurrection, they were to serve as the Foundation of the Church of Christ.

> *"Now therefore ye are no more strangers and foreigners, but fellow citizens with the saints, and of the household of God; and are built upon the foundation of the apostles and prophets, Jesus Christ himself being the chief corner stone;"* (Ephesians 2:19-20).

They brought the early church into existence and taught the disciples and converts how to become Christians. To accomplish this task, Christ gave them authority to issue commands on behalf of God.

> *"Verily I say unto you, whatsoever ye shall bind on earth shall be bound in heaven: and whatsoever ye shall loose on earth shall be loosed in heaven."* (Matthew 18:18).

So in summary, to answer the question of apostles today, we can use the word of God to judge their apostleship and evaluate how they measure up against what we know in scripture and outlined briefly here. I will add the following closing comments on this question.

By virtue of some of the tasks of the original apostles, such as writing scripture, and being the first to preach the Gospel of Jesus Christ, those who are apostles today are not one and the same as in Acts. It is a fact that some who are Apostles today have only ministered in areas and territories where the Gospel has already been preached. With that said, we have to conclude that them being called Apostles is different.

They fall into the categories of Ministries outlined in Ephesians 4:7-12, that Jesus gave at his ascension (commonly called the *5-fold ministry*). While they do not have authority to write scripture they establish churches. The foundation of the church is already established so they can only build upon that foundation. They will have more of a role of setting up and overseeing churches, performing miracles, and help to edify and perfect the church unto the measure of the stature of the fullness of Christ.

## *Question 4*

What are the Biblical Requirements to be an Apostle?

## *Answer*

The requirements for the office of an Apostle are that they were Eyewitness of Jesus' Ministry and Resurrection. Scriptures confirm this fact as follows:

> *"Wherefore of those men which have companied with us all the time that the Lord Jesus went in and out among us, beginning from the baptism of John, unto the same day, that he was taken*

*up from us, must one be ordained to be a witness with us of his Resurrection."* (Acts 1:21-22).

Paul was not one of the twelve who were called and appointed in Mark's gospel. However, Paul made it very clear how he obtained his apostleship. He went to great length to declare this in order to have standing with the rest of the Apostles.

> *"Am I not an Apostle? Am I not free? Have I not seen Jesus Christ our Lord? If I be not an apostle unto others yet doubtless, I am to you: for the seal of mine apostleship are ye in the Lord"* (I Corinthians 9:1-2).

> *"Paul a servant of Jesus Christ called to be an Apostle, separated unto the gospel of God"* (Romans 1:1).

Paul left no doubt about his apostleship and that he saw the resurrected Christ when he recounts his experience:

> *"I knew a man in Christ above fourteen years ago, (whether in the body I cannot tell; or whether out of the body, I cannot tell; God knoweth,) such an one caught up to the third heaven. Ian I knew such a man, (whether in the body, or out of the body, I cannot tell: God knoweth) how that he was caught up in Paradise, and heard unspeakable words, which it is not lawful for a man to utter."* (II Corinthians 12:2-4).

Finally, on Paul's apostolic calling, he states:

> *"Paul and Apostle (not of men, neither by man, but by Jesus Christ, and God the Father, who raised him from the dead).* (Galatians 1:1).

By referencing these scriptures, the uniqueness of the Office of the Apostle is distinguished from the gift of apostleship. Those in the Office of Apostle were given authority by Jesus Christ, to be many different things, including Establishing the Church, Writing Scriptures and Performing miracles. They are leaders of leaders, ministers of ministers and are strong spiritual influencers. The exercise of the Gift of Apostleship on the other hand involves the following:

- Planting new ministries and churches.

- Venture into places where the gospel is not preached

- Reach across cultures to establish churches and fellowship

- Venture into challenging environments

- Raise up and develop church leaders

- Call out and lead pastors and shepherds

- Establish biblical foundation for the church

- Serve as Overseers for pastors and ministries

- The Outreach ministry is a strong component of the Apostle's office

- Cross cultural ministry is an essential requirement for this office

It is not uncommon for those who operate in this gift to operate in other complimentary gifts. In fact, this gift rarely operates in isolation. Complimentary gifts are Administration, Faith, Miracles, Leadership (Governments), Evangelism.

# Question 5

Are there instances or circumstances when and individual manifests the Gift of the Spirit but their life does not exhibit or is in conflict with the Fruit of the Spirit?

# Answer

Yes. That happens more than you think and, when it does, it highlights a problem that must be addressed in the life of the individual exercising the gift. The individual who manifest the gift of the spirit should be careful to ensure their spirit (human spirit) is in subjection to and conforms to the Spirit of God. Let us pay special attention to one aspect of the Fruit of the Spirit, that of Temperance. This speaks of self-control.

The reader should note that one of the keys to the successful operation of any spiritual gift is the individual exercising the gift must have self-control. Without self-control, we have seen many persons abuse their liberty, and go overboard with exercising spiritual gifts. Note Apostle Paul addressed the matter of how to exercise control as it relates to tongues and interpretation of tongues in I Corinthians 14.

As an illustration, water undergoes a phase transition from liquid to solid, at certain temperature. Also, another phase change takes place when water is converted to steam, from liquid to gas, at another temperature. In the same way we transition from being in subjection to our human spirit to being in subjection to the Spirit of God and manifest our spiritual gift at certain times, as we are moved by the spirit. When the spirit of God has accomplished the task at hand, we transition back to our human spirit. Because we are in control of the spirit and its operation in us, some persons may choose to continue to operate as though they are being led by the spirit, even though the spirit of God is no longer in operation.

In other words, we do not make the transition from one phase to another as we expect water to make the phase change, once the temperature is reached.

Once we err in responding to the move of the Spirit of God, the result is we can cause damage to the body of Christ, and lead to confusion. When this happens, the body of Christ loses confidence in the operation of the Spirit.

To eliminate this problem, it is important that the body of Christ is taught how to manifest in their Spiritual Gift, and there is a level of maturity present in those who operate publicly in their Spiritual Gift. Immature people who operate in a spiritual gift especially the communication gifts tend to go beyond what the spirit directs and what the spirit says. It is important to stop when the spirit is lifted. There is no need to qualify what the spirit does not qualify. There is no need for addition, no need for subtraction.

Sometimes God speaks to an individual with the gift of discernment, but on a personal level. At other times, God sends a message through the individual with the gift, but aimed at the wider church body. The individual with the gift must seek wisdom to discern the difference between the two.

# Question 6

Does Psychics operate in a manner similar to how the Gift of Discerning Works?

## *Answer*

Psychics seek knowledge of the unknown by conferring with evil spirits. They sometimes devise séances and chants, practises and rituals to obtain answers from sources other than God. They may obtain such knowledge from evil spirits or by consulting with the dead.

Take special note that in the Old Testament, God prohibited his people from seeking out such knowledge. If the knowledge was obtained from God, he would not prohibit it. Here is a scripture reference:

> *"There shall not be found among you anyone that maketh his son or his daughter to pass through the fire, or that useth divination, or an observer of times, or an enchanter, or a witch."*
> (Deuteronomy 18:10).

An individual with a Spiritual Gift is able to discern between the spirit of evil and good, light and darkness, wrong and right, unspoken things, truth and error.

**Finally**, as it relates to spiritual gifts, those who are not experienced in the operation of the gift may be uncertain or doubtful about what they discern. Is it God that is showing me this? Is it just my mind? What should I do? When in doubt, be cautious. It is better to err on the side of caution. If you feel God has given you a message to be communicated to the church openly, and you have doubts or uncertainty concerning the message, it is better to hold that message and confer with your pastor, elder or minister to be sure, rather than going before the church with something that results in confusion in the body.

# CLOSING

Here are a few things to keep in mind as you continue to explore your Spiritual Gift:

1. People are naturally motivated in the area of their gifting

2. Be careful not to project your gift onto others

3. A person who is gifted in one area should resist the temptation to expect everyone else to be as motivated as they are in that particular gift

4. Be careful not to make your gifting a priority (time, commitment) for everyone else

5. Equally, those not gifted must guard against using their lack of gifting as an excuse to neglect their Christian responsibility

# REFERENCES

1  Books on Prayer. [http://www.prayerguide.org.uk/bookreviews/book.htm]. Accessed March 13, 2019.

2  CNN. The Pope, for the first time, calls the sexual abuse of nuns 'a problem.'
[http://lite.cnn.com/en/article/
h_7eaab2233a16de2385215c7c1e766d84]. Accessed February 6, 2019.

3  Dake, F. J. 1997. Dakes Annotated Reference Bible. Dake Bible Sales, Inc., Lawrenceville, Georgia.

4  Davis, J.D. 1986. Davis Dictionary of the Bible. Baker Book House, Grand Rapids, Michigan 10 PP.

5  Donavon, R.N. Concerning Spiritual Things. [https://www.sermonwriter.com/biblical-commentary/1-corinthians-121-11/]. Accessed March 2019.

6  Owen, H.L. When did the catholic church decide priests should be celibate? [https://historynewsnetwork.org/article/696]. Accessed March 2019.

7  England, M.G. 2002. An Analysis of Jesus Christ's Personality, Methodology and Teaching Style. [https://www.researchgate.

net/publication/261562464_Teaching_Methods_of_Jesus_-_
Thesis]. Accessed March 27, 2019.

8   Is there a Biblical Spiritual Gifts List? [http://www.gotques-
tions.org/spiritual-gifts-list.html]. Accessed March 5, 2019.

9   [http://www.lavistachurchofchrist.org/answers.htm]. Accessed
May 3, 2019.

10  Pytches, D. 1987. Spiritual Gifts in The Local Church. Betha-
ny House Publishers, Minneapolis, Minnesota 30 PP.

11  Spiritual Gifts Lists, Get Definitions. [http://www.mintools.
com/gifts-list.htm]. Accessed October 10, 2017.

12  Witherspoon-Toole, J. 2001. Acts: The Amazing History of the
Early Church. Pentecostal Publishing House, Hazelwood, Mo.
8 PP.

# ABOUT THE AUTHOR

Herrol Sadler commenced his Christian walk in Jamaica where he grew up in a Christian home and regularly attended Sunday School. He responded to the call to deeper study of scripture in 1987 and enrolled in the Caribbean Bible Institute, Kingston. In 2000 he graduated as Valedictorian with a Bachelor of Theology and in September of the same year, commenced a 10-year tenure as lecturer in the same institution. During this time, he taught Acts, Church History, Bible Doctrines and Christian Living. Other subjects he lectured at other institutions includes Biblical Eschatology and Christology.

He has participated extensively in the teaching ministry at Final Hour Ministries in Nassau, Bahamas and was instrumental in setting up a School of Ministry at New Life Worship Centre, and taught various subjects during the 5 years he worked in Providenciales, Turks and Caicos Island.

Now residing in Canada, Herrol is the Teaching Elder in his local church where he currently serves as the Superintendent of Sunday School. He actively teaches bible study in his local church, at conferences and special meetings mainly across Canada and occasionally in the United States.

Herrol is a Transportation Engineer by profession, and is the holder of a Bachelor's degree in Civil Engineering and a Masters degree in Transportation Engineering. He is a practicing Professional Engineer, registered in both Canada and Florida, USA. He is currently the Director of Construction with the Provincial Government of Saskatchewan, Canada.

Herrol is married to Ann-Marie, his wife of 29 years. Ann-Marie is actively involved in Ministry and is a regular speaker at conferences throughout North America and the Caribbean. Together they have 2 daughters; Sheree-Ann and Alissa.

Herrol is passionate about the Word of God and considers himself a constant student of scripture. He strongly believes that *"when a student is ready a teacher will appear."* His teaching motto is *"If the student has not learned, the teacher has not taught."*